Crash Course in Family Literacy Programs

Recent Titles in
Libraries Unlimited Crash Course Series

Crash Course in Family Literacy Programs

Rosemary Chance and Laura Sheneman

Crash Course Series

LIBRARIES UNLIMITED

AN IMPRINT OF ABC-CLIO, LLC
Santa Barbara, California • Denver, Colorado • Oxford, England

Library of Congress Cataloging-in-Publication Data

Chance, Rosemary.

  Crash course in family literacy programs / Rosemary Chance and Laura Sheneman.
    p. cm. — (Crash course)
  Includes index.
  ISBN 978-1-59884-888-5 (pbk.) — ISBN 978-1-59884-889-2 (ebook)
1. Family literacy programs—United States—Handbooks, manuals, etc.
2. Literacy—United States—Handbooks, manuals, etc.   3. Reading—Parent
participation—United States—Handbooks, manuals, etc.   I. Sheneman, Laura.
II. Title.
  LC151.C425   2012
   302.2'2440973—dc23   2011044094

ISBN: 978-1-59884-888-5
EISBN: 978-1-59884-889-2

16 15 14 13 12   1 2 3 4 5

This book is also available on the World Wide Web as an eBook.
Visit www.abc-clio.com for details.

Libraries Unlimited
An Imprint of ABC-CLIO, LLC

ABC-CLIO, LLC
130 Cremona Drive, P.O. Box 1911
Santa Barbara, California 93116-1911

This book is printed on acid-free paper ∞

Manufactured in the United States of America

CONTENTS

PREFACE AND ACKNOWLEDGMENTS

Educators recognize that quality education for children in public schools is not enough to help all children learn to read well and be academically successful. School and public librarians and teachers must extend their energy, knowledge, and expertise to include students' families. We need to broaden our horizons to embrace former First Lady Barbara Bush's view of family literacy: "The home is the child's first school, the parent is the child's first teacher, and reading is the child's first subject."

Dr. Laura Sheneman and I agree with Mrs. Bush's view wholeheartedly and wish to share our knowledge and enthusiasm for family literacy with librarians and other interested individuals. Blanche Woolls encouraged us in this endeavor, and we thank her for her support.

Our colleague Dr. Holly Weimar, an assistant professor in the department of library science at Sam Houston State University, researched family literacy and wrote chapter 4. We also had the help of Dr. Maria Magdalena Aguilar Crandall and Dr. John A. Sutterby, who have experience working with Spanish-speaking and bilingual children in south Texas. They contributed to chapter 9, and we thank them for sharing their expertise with us.

Dr. Rosemary Chance

CHAPTER 1

What Is Literacy?

"Literacy" traditionally means the ability to read and write. Reading and writing means recognizing words and being able to write words in a sentence. In the 21st century, literacy has taken on multiple meanings other than the ability to read and write. The National Literacy Act of 1991 defined literacy as "an individual's ability to read, write, and speak English, and compute and solve problems at levels of proficiency necessary to function on the job and in society, to achieve one's goals and develop ones' knowledge and potential" (Wasik, 2004, p. 4). This definition encompasses many possibilities wrapped up in the word "literacy." In 2005 the American Library Association adopted a literacy definition that is almost identical. For the purpose of understanding the possibilities of literacy and what it means to be literate, let's view literacy through two lenses: stages of literary appreciation and know-how.

VIEWING LITERACY THROUGH SIX STAGES OF LITERARY APPRECIATION

Viewing literacy through six stages of literary appreciation highlights the variety of needs, reading interests, and approaches unique to children, adolescents, and adults. The focus on literacy begins at the first two stages, birth through kindergarten and kindergarten through second grade. These two stages are often referred to as emerging literacy as babies and young children begin to understand oral language and discover the significance of letters and the meanings of words and sentences. Kenneth L. Donelson and Aileen Pace Nilsen, experts in the field of youth literature, describe six stages of literary appreciation that people move through on their way to becoming life-long readers: birth through kindergarten; kindergarten through second grade; third through sixth grade; junior high school and high school; upper high school and college; and adulthood (2004, pp. 38–43).

These stages will overlap, of course. For instance, adults may read Shakespeare and the poetry of Emily Dickinson for the aesthetic appreciation but then also enjoy crime mysteries, romances, and biographies. For those who have not experienced literacy at the first two stages, the focus changes to trying to get these adults into a program to help them become literate. Let's start at the beginning with definitions of how children become literate.

Birth through kindergarten—During the earliest period of life children enjoy nursery rhymes, board books, folktales, picture books, moveable books, pop-up books, and anything in their world that shows them that letters and words are useful and fun.

Kindergarten through second grade—Young children focus on decoding words and sentences. They practice their newly acquired reading skills through early readers, through classic titles, such as *The Cat in the Hat* by Dr. Seuss, and through a series of readers, such as Mr. Putter and Tabby. Picture storybooks, such as *Peter's Chair* by Ezra Jack Keats and *Where the Wild Things Are* by Maurice Sendak, can further their enjoyment of reading and connecting text with illustration.

Third through sixth grade—If children can find a book of such interest that they lose themselves in the story or narrative, then they are well on their way to becoming life-long readers. The books that bring them unconscious delight could be series books, fantasies, horse stories, dog stories, adventure tales, informational books, or any reading that intrigues them enough to read for pure enjoyment. Once a child experiences this type of pleasurable reading, they will want to read more and more.

Junior high school and high school—These students may be termed "teens," "young adults," or "adolescents." They want to find themselves in stories. They want to find their friends, their enemies, others teens like them, and other people of interest. They may select a variety of fiction, poetry, biography, and informational books. They usually like to read realistic stories, mysteries, and humor.

Even though students who cannot read at grade level might be considered lacking in literacy, most consider someone who cannot read in upper high school as illiterate. Helping adults learn to read is not the focus of this book, but in planning family literacy programs librarians must be aware that there will be some adults who cannot read. Literary appreciation stages for high school and beyond are defined here.

Upper high school and college—Older teens and the youngest adults move beyond egocentric concerns to the broader society. They question society and the world around them. They wonder where and how they fit in. They may read controversial books, including books that reveal contemporary problems and dilemmas.

Adulthood—Reading for sophisticated pleasure means appreciating the author's writing style, being touched by the story, and admiring the intellect, the research, and the skill of the author to write fiction, poetry, and informational books so brilliantly. Classic works include Harper Lee's *To Kill a Mockingbird*, William Golding's *Lord of the Flies*, the poetry of Maya Angelou, Emily Dickinson, and Robert Frost, among countless others.

VIEWING LITERACY THROUGH KNOW-HOW

Besides knowing how to read and write, literacy includes specific skills and knowledge. Thus the coining of multiple literacies, such as computer, cultural, digital, financial, health, information, math, media, and visual. Each literacy type assumes a cognitive knowledge and an acquisition of specific skills. In today's world, certain of these skills are acquired in the process of learning to read, write, and speak English and are part of a child's formal education. Computer, math, and visual literacies can be integrated informally into early life and are part of traditional school life. In schools, students at every level have access to technology labs and to libraries with computers. Teachers are encouraged to integrate technology into their lessons so that even very young children have a basic knowledge of how computers work and how they can be used.

Adults are very much in need of financial and health literacy. If they aren't frequent users of the Internet, they need to learn how to find such information. Adults often acquire their computer literacy as a part of programming in the public library. Older adults particularly enjoy being able to "converse" online with family members, especially grandchildren, and they often come to the public library for computer training.

Visual literacy is a particularly interesting area. While there are no specific courses for teaching visual literacy, books and other print and digital resources can strengthen a child's skill in this area. Young children are naturally visually oriented and can recognize common objects and animals in pictures: cat, dog, apple, tree, and so forth. Board books, wordless books, and picture books have a natural attraction to emerging readers. Images can reinforce and enrich textual concepts throughout a child's education. Picture book illustrations and photographs, charts, maps, and tables in informational books of all reading levels contribute to increasing readers' skill at interpreting visual elements. Being able to correctly interpret visual aids in books and online is a skill that extends throughout school years and into adult workplaces.

VARIABLES OF LITERACY DEVELOPMENT

Literacy is a complex mix of knowledge, skills, and environment. When considering how best to help our first group, children, achieve basic levels of literacy, it makes sense to pay attention to the variables that can influence a child's literacy development.

1. Social aspects. Do adults in the home speak meaningfully with the child? Young children begin the foundation for literacy at home with parents, other family members, and friends who can help show them the world they have entered by talking with them, naming objects, and sharing their environment.
2. Cultural aspects. What ethnic or racial culture does the child experience? Young children are immediately immersed in the environment of their family's culture, whether from a distinct section of the United States or from a particular cultural ethnicity.
3. Second language. Does the family speak a language other than English? Children may grow up in a home where English is not spoken or written.
4. Book-related activities. Are books easily accessible to the child? In homes where books are plentiful, reading is modeled by family members, and stories are read aloud, children have an ideal opportunity to advance their literacy.
5. Importance of libraries. Does the family regularly visit a library? Access to school and public libraries (and the large collections of books and other media in them) from an early age throughout high school can influence children's literacy development.
6. Economic status. Are the child's basic needs met? Does she have food, shelter, clothing, and love? Children whose parents can provide the basic needs and advantages beyond basic needs have the best chance of becoming readers. When families make trips to libraries, museums, and other locations that stimulate children's' curiosity and imagination, children will be better prepared to read. With exposure to positive life experiences, they will have the background to understand what they are reading.
7. Education level of parents. What is the level of the parents' education? Parents who are well-educated potentially have confidence in themselves and knowledge of the world, and they provide models their children can aspire to.
8. Technology opportunities. Is technology available to the child? The availability of computers in homes allow children opportunities for exploring their world, finding information, interacting with people from diverse cultures, reading online, and staying current with technological development.

A BRIEF HISTORICAL VIEW OF LITERACY SEEN THROUGH A PROGRESSION OF BOOKS FOR YOUTH

In the 21st century, the focus for literacy begins with children, and most family literacy programs are started in the schools although a child's first experience with books and reading may start in the public library. Viewing literacy through a brief history of books for youth places emphasis on a primary tool of literacy: children's and young adults' available reading material. Significant titles across six centuries reflect societal changes in thoughts about children, education, and literacy. Beginning with the 15th century, Johannes Gutenberg's invention of the printing press with moveable type changed the world by making printed books available to all people. William Caxton introduced printing to England in 1476 and printed two tales with appeal to children: *Reynard the Fox* (1481) and *The Fables of Aesop* (1484).

In the 1400s in England hornbooks were produced to provide school children with the alphabet, the syllables, and the Lord's Prayer. These were not the book format of today but were instead books fashioned from a piece of wood in the shape of a paddle and then layered with hand-printed paper and a thin sheet of translucent horn to protect the paper. The paper and the thin protective sheet were secured to the wooden paddle by narrow strips of brass around the edges of the paddle and were held down by small nails. Hornbooks were common until the 18th century when battledores, a folded cardboard format with similar content, took their place. In the 1500s chapbooks, popular works sold for a few pence, began a rise to popularity that continued through the 1800s. Peddlers in Europe and America sold these short, cheap books that were based on legends, ballads, supernatural stories, and religious instruction. Stories based on ballads and traditional tales, such as "Jack the Giant Killer" and "Tom Thumb," were favorites and became the forerunners to western stories and comic books.

In 1657 a Czech educator, John Amos Comenius, completed *Orbis Sensualium Pictus*, or "Visible World." *Orbis Sensualium Pictus* is considered by experts in the field of children's literature to be the first picture book for children, the first illustrated informational book for children, and a precursor to encyclopedias. This illustrated book introduced the importance of visual literacy into the field of children's literature.

Education and religion were featured together in *The New England Primer* (1690), a combination of alphabet studies and catechism, designed to teach reading and Puritan ideals (Norton, 1999). With the publication of John Locke's *Some Thoughts Concerning Education* (1693), the view adults had of children changed. Locke regarded children's minds as blank pages to be filled rather than the previous view of children as small adults. From Locke's philosophy, an important realization "dawned that children might benefit from books written to encourage their reading" (Norton, 1999, p. 68). Charles Perrault's *Tales of Mother Goose* (1698) featured well-known fairy tales, such as "Cinderella," "Sleeping Beauty," "Puss in Boots," and "Little Red Riding Hood." Perrault's collection was written specifically for the amusement of children.

18th- and 19th-Century Books for Youth

Besides books about education, religion, and folktales; adventure stories, poetry, and stories of real children were published in the 18th century. Although *Robinson Crusoe* (1719) by Daniel Defoe was written for adults, children, skipping sections about religion and moralizing, read it for the adventure and the clever survival strategies. In

1744 book entrepreneur John Newbery published Oliver Goldsmith's *History of Little Goody Two Shoes*. This marked the beginning of books that were designed to be attractive to children. Newbery's success lead to his fame as a promoter of children's books; and the first children's book award is named after him.

During the 19th century we begin to see true development of literature for young people: poetry, fantasy, illustrated books, stories of other countries, realistic fiction, science fiction, family stories, and more adventure stories. Poetry published especially for children became popular: "Twinkle, Twinkle, Little Star" (1804) by Jane Taylor; "The Night before Christmas" (1823) by Clement Clarke Moore; "Mary Had a Little Lamb" (1830) by Sarah Josepha Hale; *A Book of Nonsense* (1846) by Edward Lear, *Sing-Song* (1872) by Christina Rossetti, and *A Child's Garden of Verses* (1885) by Robert Louis Stevenson.

At the end of the century more attention was being paid to book illustration than in previous years. Walter Crane, Randolph Caldecott, and Kate Greenaway were British artists credited with beginning the emphasis on quality illustrations in children's books. Their use of color and their skillful artwork resulted in beauty in illustration not seen before. Walter Crane, a wood engraver, is considered by some experts in the field of children's literature the father of illustration for children. From 1865 to 1876 he illustrated a series of nursery picture books and fairy tales, including *The House that Jack Built* (1865), *This Pig Went to Market*, and *Beauty and the Beast* (Meigs, Eaton, Nesbitt, & Viguers, 1969, p. 230). In 1938, Randolph Caldecott was honored for his illustration brilliance by having an American Library Association (ALA) award named after him. Caldecott's *The Diverting History of John Gilpin*, his first in a series of picture books, is especially lauded for its humor and characters in action, another change from previous illustrations. Kate Greenaway's illustrations feature flowers and scenes from the countryside where she lived as a child. *Under the Window* (1878) was her first picture book, showing children at school and at play.

Fairy tales continued to be popular, especially *Grimm's German Popular Stories* (1823), tales collected in Germany and published in multiple volumes translated into English by Jacob and Wilhelm Grimm. Hans Christian Andersen of Denmark created original fairy tales, rewrote some he knew from his childhood, and published a collection entitled *Fairy Tales Told for Children* (1846). Gradually, a sense of fun was slipping into stories and poetry for children. Lewis Carroll's *Alice's Adventures in Wonderland* (1865) is filled with imaginative scenes and characters imbued with nonsense and with no moralizing. Some of the most popular adventure stories were written during the end of the 19th century. Jules Verne's *Twenty Thousand Leagues under the Sea* (1869) marked the beginning of science fiction. More earthly adventures include Robert Louis Stevenson's *Treasure Island* (1883); *The Merry Adventures of Robin Hood* (1883), collected and illustrated by Robert Pyle; and Mark Twain's *The Adventures of Huckleberry Finn* (1884). Significant realistic family stories written by women were published along with the fantastic and humorous ones: Martha Finley's *Elsie Dinsmore* (1867), Louisa May Alcott's *Little Women* (1868), and Margaret Sidney's *The Five Little Peppers and How They Grew* (1880). Two stories set in other countries that were popular in America in the late 1880s and remain popular classics today are: Mary Mapes Dodge's *Hans Brinker or the Silver Skates* (set in Holland) and Johanna Spyri's *Heidi* (set in Switzerland; 1884).

20th-Century Books for Youth

In the 20th century, numerous wonderful books were published for children and teens. Below is a small sampling of books for youth, limited to picture books and fiction. Some are winners of the Randolph Caldecott Medal, established in 1938. Some are winners of the John Newbery Medal, established in 1922. All of the books listed have stayed in print and are considered classic titles today. More titles of winners can be located through the ALA Web page at http://www.ala.org.

Picture Books

Tale of Peter Rabbit by Beatrix Potter (1901)
Millions of Cats by Wanda Gag (1928)
The Story of Babar by Jean de Brunhof (1933)
Madeline by Ludwig Bemelmans (1939)
The Cat and the Hat by Dr. Seuss (Theodore Geisel) (1957)
Where the Wild Things Are by Maurice Sendak (1963)
The Snowy Day by Ezra Jack Keats (1963)
Why Mosquitoes Buzz in People's Ears by Leo and Diane Dillon (1975)
The Polar Express by Chris Van Allsburg (1985)
Black and White by David Macaulay (1990)
Rapunzel by Paul O. Zelinsky (1997)
Olivia by Ian Falconer (2000)

Fiction

The Wonderful World of Oz by L. Frank Baum (1900)
Just So Stories by Rudyard Kipling (1902)
Rebecca of Sunnybrook Farm by Kate Douglas Wiggin (1904)
Anne of Green Gables by Lucy Maud Montgomery (1908)
The Secret Garden by Frances Hodgson Burnett (1910)
The Hobbit by J.R.R. Tolkien (1937)
Johnny Tremain by Esther Forbes (1943)
A Tree Grows in Brooklyn by Betty Smith (1943)
Hot Rod by Henry Felson (1950)
The Catcher in the Rye by J.D. Salinger (1951)
Charlotte's Web by E.B. White (1952)
The Lion, the Witch and the Wardrobe by C.S. Lewis (1961)
Are You There, God? It's Me, Margaret by Judy Blume (1970)
M.C. Higgins, the Great by Virginia Hamilton (1973)
The Giver by Lois Lowry (1993)
Holes by Louis Sachar (1998)
Stuck in Neutral by Terry Trueman (2000)

It may seem strange to list and describe books for youth in a chapter on literacy rather than listing specific reading skills. It would seem even stranger to a librarian not to emphasize significant books throughout our history. Continuing in that vein, a brief sampling of awards for authors, illustrators, and their books also seems appropriate.

AWARDS FOR AUTHORS, ILLUSTRATORS, AND BOOKS

Focusing on the importance of libraries in the development of literacy, it seems like a natural step to point out a sampling of book awards, types of books, and titles that have the potential to impact literacy development for youth. Book awards immediately provide a pathway to quality and popular literature. Parents and librarians can select recommended books for prekindergarten emerging readers through high school readers. Hundreds of awards are given for young people's books. Awards are sponsored by foreign countries, individual states, and organizations, such as the ALA, the National Council of Teachers of English (NCTE), and the International Reading Association (IRA), among others. The following 20 book awards and book lists are among the most prestigious and well-known book awards for youth in the United States.

1. The Asian/Pacific American Award for Literature (APAAL) honors works for children, young adults, and adults that promote the culture and heritage of Asian/Pacific Americans and is sponsored by the Asian/Pacific American Library Association (APALA).
2. The Children's Choices consists of an annual list of about 100 books voted on by children in five regions of the United States and is sponsored by the International Reading Association.
3. The Coretta Scott King Book Award honors writers and illustrators of African American heritage who write and illustrate books for children and young adults focused on African American experiences. The award is sponsored by ALA.
4. The Edgars are given for the best mysteries published during the year in a range of categories, including juvenile, young adult, and adult. The awards honor Edgar Allan Poe and are sponsored by the Mystery Writers of America.
5. The Hans Christian Andersen Award honors a living author and a living illustrator for their body of work and is presented by the International Board on Books for Young People (IBBY).
6. The Jane Addams Children's Book Awards honor books for children ages 2–12 that "effectively promote the cause of peace, social justice, world community, and the equality of the sexes and all races as well as meeting conventional standards for excellence," according to the website of the Jane Addams Peace Association, sponsor of the awards.
7. The John Newbery Medal, the oldest children book award in the world, honors the most distinguished book of the year for children up to and including age 14. The

award is sponsored by the American Association of Library Services to Children (ALSC), a division of ALA.

8. The Laura Ingalls Wilder Medal honors an author or illustrator whose books have made a lasting and substantial contribution to children's literature. The award is given once every three years and is sponsored by ALSC.

9. The Michael L. Printz Award honors the most distinguished book published in English during the previous year for young adults ages 12–18 and is sponsored by the Young Adult Library Services Association (YALSA), a division of ALA.

10. The Mildred Batchelder Award honors an American publisher for a children's book considered to be the most outstanding of those books originally published in a language other than English in a country other than the United States, and subsequently translated into English and published in the United States.

11. The Award for Excellence in Children's Poetry honors a living American poet for his or her body of work for children. The award is given every three years by the NCTE.

12. The Notable Children's Books list is an annual list of the best books for children, birth through age 14, and chosen by a committee of librarians, sponsored by ALSC.

13. The Orbis Pictus Award for Outstanding Nonfiction for Children honors the author of an excellent nonfiction book for children in grades K through 8. The award is sponsored by NCTE.

14. The Pura Belpré Award honors a Latino/Latina writer and illustrator whose work best portrays, affirms, and celebrates the Latino cultural experience in an outstanding work of literature for children and youth. The award is sponsored jointly by ALA and the National Association to Promote Library Services to the Spanish Speaking (REFORMA), an ALA Affiliate.

15. The Randolph Caldecott Medal honors the artist of the most distinguished American picture book for children. The award is sponsored by the ALA.

16. The Robert Sibert Informational Book Medal honors the author(s) and illustrator(s) of the most distinguished informational books published in English. The award is sponsored by ALA.

17. The Scott O'Dell Award for Historical Fiction honors the author of distinguished historical fiction for youth set in the New World (North, South, or Central America). The award was established by Scott O'Dell, a Newbery Award–winning author.

18. The Theodore Seuss Geisel Award honors the author(s) and illustrator(s) of the most distinguished American book for beginning readers published in English in the United States.

19. The Tomás Rivera Mexican American Children's Book Award honors authors and illustrators who depict the Mexican American experience in quality literature for young people. The award honors Tomás Rivera, a distinguished alumnus of Texas State University in San Marcos, Texas.

20. The Young Adults' Choices award list is of a list of 30 books chosen by middle school and high school students in five regions across the United States. The award list is sponsored by IRA.

CONCLUSION

As our society advances, we recognize that being literate is essential to functioning well in the United States. The basic abilities to read and write, including competencies in multiple literacies, are essential. Understanding stages of literacy and variables of literacy development is essential. Recognizing the importance and availability of reading materials for every age level is essential. For librarians in school and public libraries, knowing and selecting classical and contemporary titles is an essential skill for helping children, teens, and adults to advance their own literacy.

References

Donelson, K. L., & Nilsen, A. P. (2004). *Literature for today's young adults* (7th ed.). Boston, MA: Pearson.

Meigs, C., Eaton, A. T., Nesbitt, E., & Viguers, R. H. (1969). *A critical history of children's literature* (Rev. ed.). London: Macmillan.

Norton, D. (1999). *Through the eyes of a child* (5th ed.). Upper Saddle River, NJ: Merrill.

Wasik, B. H. (Ed.). (2004). *Handbook of family literacy*. Mahwah, NJ: Lawrence Erlbaum Associates.

CHAPTER 2

What Is Family Literacy?

At the heart of family literacy is the improvement of reading and writing skills for children and parents in one family. Initiatives to improve family literacy are considered educational methods seeking to improve children's overall academic performance through family involvement. If parents understand and implement child-parent interactions related to literacy, they can make a significant positive impact on the lives of their children.

For this book, the example of a program from Texas is used to illustrate one family literacy program. Former First Lady Barbara Bush states her view of family literacy: "The home is the child's first school, the parent is the child's first teacher, and reading is the child's first subject" (http://www.barbarabushfoundation.com). In recent years, literacy experts have recognized that child-parent relationships are essential to the development of a child's literacy ability. As a result of this recognition, family literacy initiatives have become a popular method to positively impact the literacy skills of families and, ultimately, those of children. Public and school libraries are common settings for these family literacy initiatives in the form of carefully planned programs and events.

Public librarians begin with the experiences they offer during story time at the library. Literacy begins there with lap sit programs where parents can bring their children at a very young age to be introduced to stories and to encourage parents to take board books home to share. These programs continue, and children are given basic reading readiness experiences. For more information please see the Every Child Ready to Read program, sponsored by the Association of Library Services for Children and the Public Library Association, divisions of the American Library Association, at http://www.everychildreadytoread.org.

WHO IS AFFECTED MOST BY THE LACK OF LITERACY?

Understanding who is affected most by the lack of literacy will lead us to what issues and concerns should be addressed in any family literacy initiative. Three groups of people in the United States are most affected by illiteracy or limited literacy: the working poor, female heads of households, and minority groups, including people who speak and/or read a primary language other than English. In turn, these three groups of adults impact the literacy of their children. Each group has three characteristics in common: limited income, low literacy competencies, and low education levels.

An examination of the U.S. Census Bureau's figures from the 2009 American Community Survey (2009 Survey; http://www.factfinder.census.gov) sheds light on the plight of these groups. Statistics from the 2009 Survey provide data on specific geographic locations and specific populations in the United States, including people in poverty, female heads of households, and people of a wide range of ethnic and racial diversity.

The fastest-growing minority group in the United States is the Hispanic/Latino population. According to the 2009 Survey, the U.S. population is slightly over 307 million. The Hispanic/Latino population is almost 48.5 million, or one-sixth of the U.S. population. Viewing the Hispanic/Latino population statistics and comparing them to overall U.S. population statistics dramatically shows the barriers a minority population faces. For example, of 113.5 million households, 12.5 million households are headed by Hispanic/Latino women. Of those women 12.5% have children under 18 years old. Further, 49% of Hispanic/Latino women who head households and have children below 5 years old live in poverty. The percentage of Hispanic/Latino children under 18 and living in poverty is 26.4% of the Hispanic/Latino population compared to 16.6% of the overall U.S. population. Spanish speakers comprise 76.2% of the Hispanic/Latino population 5 years old and over. More than 26 million (39.1%) Hispanic/Latino people 25 years and older have less than a high school diploma (http://www.factfinder.census.gov). The combination of growing numbers of minority children in poverty who only speak Spanish and whose parents have less than a high school education adds up to a major educational challenge for the United States.

Being poor, uneducated, and a limited English speaker in America has unavoidable implications. These implications affect the literacy development of children and their future educational success. Typically, these implications about the family become barriers to literacy:

1. Homes have few or no books for children to read. Parents may not be able to afford to purchase books, and they may not realize the importance of introducing books to children at an early age.
2. Parents may not be readers, and thus, they don't model reading for their children. They don't communicate either directly or through their actions the importance and pleasure of reading.
3. Easy access to transportation is not available for taking children to the public library or to other educational experiences such as trips to museums, zoos, or locations outside their own neighborhoods or cities.
4. Parents may not be comfortable going to their children's schools because of a language barrier or discomfort in meeting teachers and administrators. They may not have transportation during the day for going to the schools for teacher/parent conferences, or they may not be able to leave their jobs to attend a conference.
5. Parents may have limited access to other parents of children who attend the same school. There may not be other parents to talk with who understand the American education system.

Although all parents and their children are invited to school and public library family literacy events and can benefit from them, few are able to attend. Families living in poverty and families who have limited English language competencies are the major target population.

WHAT IS A FAMILY LITERACY PROGRAM?

A family literacy program is a carefully planned sequence of events and meetings with availability to resources that are helpful to a family. This program seeks to address the literacy needs of parents and children. A few examples of successful family literacy programs follow with more details available in later chapters. While many of the programs cited below are started in schools, public librarians need to be aware of these possibilities and make sure that, if any one of them is offered in the school, the public librarian can offer to help as much as possible.

The largest national initiative, Even Start, adheres to four program initiatives according to its *Guide to Quality* (2001):

1. Interactive literacy activities between parents and their children.
2. Training for parents regarding how to be the primary teacher for their children and full partners in the education of their children.
3. Adult education and training that leads to personal growth and economic self-sufficiency.

4. Age-appropriate education for children to prepare them for success in school and in life (p. 26).

Sharon Darling, an expert in family literacy, suggests that the success of national literacy programs depends upon specific factors. These factors should be considered as well when working with more limited state and local programs.

1. A primary motivator for family participation is the "parents' desire for their children to succeed" (Darling, 2004, p. 608).
2. A program's success depends upon it being well implemented.
3. Staff development opportunities should be available to train teachers and volunteers how to work with families.
4. Programs should offer more work-related instruction, more flexible scheduling, and more child care.
5. Policies for staffing and for improving collaboration among funding and supporting agencies should be clearly stated.

Second, Prime Time Family Reading Time is a literacy program that began as a state program and has grown into a national one. Prime Time, a program developed by the Louisiana Endowment for the Humanities (LEH) in 1991, is "a unique six-week humanities-based program of reading, discussion, and storytelling at public libraries and other venues" (Louisiana Endowment for the Humanities [LEH], n.d.). This state-wide program is designed to empower "parents/guardians with low literacy skills and/ or limited English language abilities to help their children, ages 6–10, enjoy reading and improve their reading abilities" (LEH, n.d.). The focus of the program is to reach out to underserved families, such as the growing Latino population in DeKalb County, Georgia (Deeds, 2009, p. 29). Carefully developed methods and materials and evidence of successful results make Prime Time a vital program to be considered in every state. Currently, Prime Time flourishes in 38 states and the Virgin Islands. Funding provides training for storytellers, humanities scholars, and coordinators of local programs in addition to some transportation for participants, certificates of completion, and gift books (LEH, n.d.).

Third, local family literacy programs in schools share some goals with programs such as Even Start and Prime Time that are often held in public libraries. Obviously, schools are expected to provide age-appropriate education for children, including learning to read and to appreciate books. Typically, schools do not provide language and job training for parents, although there are exceptions where the population of the school and its community are predominantly one ethnicity or race. Schools may offer after-school, evening, and/or Saturday programs that provide interactive literacy lessons and training for parents. Most family literacy programs target emerging readers, those children in kindergarten through second grade. Programs may also target children in upper elementary grades, adjusting activities and offering book titles to fit the students' needs.

Typically, family literacy programs for elementary children are offered more frequently than programs for older students. In middle schools a major family literacy program may be offered only once a semester. In high schools and middle schools, family literacy programs are most likely to take the form of book clubs that involve parents as well as students.

Public libraries often have mother-daughter book clubs or father-son book clubs because they work well without interfering with the school curriculum or activities. For great ideas about book clubs in both school and public libraries, refer to *The Teen-Centered Book Club: Readers into Leaders* by Bonnie Kunzel and Constance Hardesty (2006). Details about school family literacy programs for elementary children are available in later chapters in this book.

WHAT ARE THE BENEFITS OF FAMILY LITERACY PROGRAMS?

The benefits of family literacy programs are somewhat obvious although their success depends upon certain factors. Obviously, the major expectations of programs are the improvement of reading skills and academic achievement for children. There may be side benefits, depending upon the scope of a particular program. Large programs like Even Start have the potential to:

1. Improve socioeconomic levels of families;
2. Help parents better understand the American education system and the roles of teachers and librarians;
3. Make parents aware of social services available to them;
4. Improve English language skills for both children and parents;
5. Improve parenting knowledge and skills.

WHAT IS THE ROLE OF PARENTS IN FAMILY LITERACY PROGRAMS?

Depending upon the educational offerings and expectations of a program, parents obviously play an essential role in the success of a family literacy program.

1. Parents provide transportation to and from programs.
2. Parents provide enthusiasm and motivation for children to attend programs.
3. At home, parents use teaching methods and learning activities they have learned from attending programs.
4. Parents provide arrangements and support for consistently attending programs.

WHAT IS THE ROLE OF LIBRARIANS IN FAMILY LITERACY PROGRAMS?

As professionals, either in schools or public libraries, the specific features and parameters of a particular program will define the role of librarians. In large programs such as Even Start, a librarian may be one of the grant writers; and in local school programs, the librarian may have the responsibility of planning a program with or without consultation with teachers and administrators. Thus, librarians may be responsible for:

1. Planning programs;
2. Advertising programs;
3. Choosing guest readers and storytellers;
4. Choosing specific activities for parent and child interaction;
5. Selecting books to be read and shared during an event;
6. Arranging lessons for parenting education, especially related to books and reading.

CONCLUSION

To improve family literacy, there are programs and help available at local, state, and national levels. Keep in mind that the strategy of a program is to teach and encourage child-parent interactions with reading and books. Two critical questions, posed by Darling (2004), can help guide planners of family literacy programs: "What is the need for family literacy services and programs? Is the need likely to continue?" (p. 604).

References

Darling, S. (2004). Future directions for family literacy. In B. H. Wasik (Ed.), *Handbook of family literacy* (pp. 603–616). Mahwah, NJ: Lawrence Erlbaum Associates.

Deeds, S. (2009). Ready for Prime Time? One library's experience with the humanities program. *Children and Libraries*, 7(2), 29–31.

Guide to quality: Even Start Family Literacy Program. (2001). Washington, DC: U.S. Department of Education.

Louisiana Endowment for the Humanities (LEH). (n.d.). Prime Time Family Reading Time. Retrieved from http://www.leh.org/html/primetime.html

CHAPTER 3

Who Funds Family Literacy Programs?

Programs throughout the United States are funded by the federal government, through individual state initiatives, regional and city/town literacy councils, and school districts. Knowing who funds a particular family literacy program leads to understanding specific application criteria and understanding funding amounts and how funding works. In this chapter, topics include basic understanding of grant applications and basic advice for completing a successful grant application. A list of major literacy programs is provided. More information about these programs can be found throughout the chapters of this book and through their Web pages. Please be aware that funding for literacy programs fluctuates and may have altered since the writing of this book.

MAJOR FAMILY LITERACY PROGRAMS

As stated in chapter 2, the Barbara Bush program in Texas is used as a model for family literacy programs. Programs for librarians in other states are also listed.

Barbara Bush Foundation for Family Literacy (BBFFL) includes national grants and state literacy initiatives. The First Lady's Family Initiative for Texas (FLFIT) includes a Program Implementation grant and a Planning Implementation grant (http://www.barbarabushfoundation.com/).

Funding for Program Implementation, 2011: $50,000
Funding for Planning Implementation, 2011: $5,000

Even Start Family Literacy Program is the largest federal grant program for family literacy programs in the United States and "offers grants to support local family literacy projects that integrate early childhood education, adult literacy, parenting education, and interactive parent and child literacy activities for low-income families" (www2.ed.gov/programs/evenstartformula/index.html).

Estimated range of awards in 2010: $30,632–$7,154,872 (www2.ed.gov/programs/evenstartformula/funding.html)

The Family and Child Education Program (FACE) was initiated in 1990 as "an early childhood/parental involvement program for American Indian families" in Bureau of Indian Education (BIE)–funded schools. As of June 9, 2010, FACE has literacy programs in 44 BIE funded schools (http://www.faceresources.org/).

Improving Literacy through School Libraries (LSL). "This program helps LEAs [local education agencies] improve reading achievement by providing increased access to up-to-date library materials; a well-equipped, technologically advanced school library media center; and well-trained, professionally certified school library media specialists" (www2.gov.edu/programs/lsl/index.html).

Range of awards in 2010: $30,000–$500,000 (www2.ed.gov/programs/lsl/funding.html)

National Center for Family Literacy (NCFL) provides an encompassing umbrella for model literacy programs, such as the Toyota Family Literacy Program and the Better World Books/NCFL Libraries and Families Award, intended "to reward and enhance existing family literacy programs and to expand literacy-building practices of families in library settings" (http://www.famlit.org/award-grant-opportunties/bwb-award/).

Award grants in 2010 for Better World Books/NCFL Libraries and Families Award: three at $10,000 each

Prime Time Family Reading Time was created by the Louisiana Endowment for the Humanities in 1991 to reach out to low literacy and non-English speaking members of the community through public libraries. The program is "an award-winning reading, discussion, and storytelling series based on illustrated children's books. National expansion is made possible through a grant from the National Endowment for the Humanities and is a cooperative endeavor with the ALA Public Programs Office" (http://atyourlibrary.org/prime-time-family-literacy).

Award value estimated at approximately: $60,000

Toyota Family Literacy Program (TFLP) was created in 1991 and was the first program created to benefit Hispanic families. Toyota has contributed millions of dollars to NCFL to help create programs in cities throughout the United States. As of May 11, 2010, TFLP had funded programs in 50 cities and 30 states, including three elementary schools in Patterson, California, where a $600,000 grant funds literacy programs for Hispanics and other immigrant families (http://pressroomtoyota.com/pr/tms/national-literacy-program-unveiled-158414.aspx).

BASIC UNDERSTANDINGS OF GRANT APPLICATIONS

Making sure that you understand all aspects of a grant application may seem like an obvious action, but grant applications have specific details that must be adhered to if you want to be successful in your application, in the implementation of the grant, and in the desired results of the grant. This chapter is not intended to be a comprehensive view of grant applications but rather to provide some advice related to literacy grants and how they work. Examples of understandings come from the BBFFL and from the FLFIT in Texas, 2011–2012.

1. Understand what the grant is for and that requirements may have changed from the previous year. For example, the BBFFL Program Implementation grants given to organizations in Texas provide for four choices:
   a. help create a family literacy program
   b. expand an existing reading program
   c. allow for an innovative project
   d. replicate a successful family literacy program

2. Understand that large grants usually require partner organizations. Sometimes other grants, such as Title I, and programs, such as Head Start, are partners. For instance, TFLP is a model program of NCFL. Toyota provides funding and NCFL provides the model for multicultural family literacy education.

3. Understand that grants are awarded to nonprofit organizations only. Public libraries and public school districts are considered nonprofit; private schools and charter schools are considered for-profit organizations. (Note: For-profit organizations can seek funds elsewhere, such as through foundations or private benefactors.)

4. Understand that some grants require matching funds from the budget or fund-raising activities or in-kind contributions, non-cash items, such as the use of a teacher, a classroom, and a vehicle.

5. Understand what funding pays for and what it does not pay for. In the case of the FLFIT, funding allows reasonable costs for meals and snacks as well as "costs for training, testing materials, conferences, grant orientation meeting, and outside evaluation" (http://www.tcall.tamu.edu/bbush/impgrant2011.html).

6. Understand when funding is paid. For instance, the FLFIT application states that 50% of the funding is disbursed at start-up of the program, 25% after the first report is submitted, and 25% after reports are received and reviewed (http://www-tcall. tamu.edu/bbush/impgrant2011.html).
7. Understand who is required to participate in the services of the grant. The FLFIT requires the inclusion of children ages birth through third grade.
8. Understand that formal assessment of the results of the grant may be required. The FLFIT requires the Texas Primary Reading Inventory for assessment of school-age children.
9. Understand the application evaluation criteria. A competitive review of the FLFIT criteria are shown as follows:

Section Points

Organization's background and need for the project	20
Project design	30
Recruitment and retention	20
Project outcomes and assessment	10
Program management and staff qualifications	10
Collaboration, community support, and project site	10
TOTAL	100

BASIC ADVICE FOR COMPLETING A SUCCESSFUL GRANT APPLICATION

Some of the advice that follows may seem obvious, but strict adherence to grant application guidelines can make the difference between winning a grant and being turned down. Federal grants, like Even Start, and state grants, such as grants given through the BBFFL, are highly competitive. In 2010 in Texas, only nine grantees were chosen out of 300 applications for a BBFFL Literacy Implementation Grant. Something as simple as forgetting to include an authorized signature on a cover sheet can eliminate an application. Because the amount of funding for a particular grant may be substantial, it's critical that every piece of the grant application is addressed accurately. In the case of the BBFFL Program Implementation grants for 2011–2012, a grant award may be as much as $50,000.

1. Read application guidelines carefully.
2. Follow application guidelines exactly. There are FAQs on the BBFFL Web page. Some of the questions that are frequently asked are ones that are already clearly addressed in the guidelines related to authorized signature on cover sheet, etc.
3. Follow the required delivery method. For instance, a completed application for the FLFIT must be submitted as an e-mail attachment; the signed cover sheet may be faxed or scanned and sent as an e-mail attachment.

4. Adhere to the time period of the grant. For example, in 2011–2012, eligible programs for the FLFIT start by September 15, 2011, and end between May 31 and July 31, 2012.

For more information about successfully applying for grants, an excellent resource is *Winning Grants: A How-To-Do-It Manual for Librarians with Multimedia Tutorials and Grant Development* by Pamela H. MacKellar and Stephanie K. Gerding, 2010, and *Librarian's Handbook for Seeking, Writing, and Managing Grants* by Sylvia D. Hall-Ellis and others, 2011.

BASICS OF LOCAL FUNDING

Family literacy programs can contribute significantly to the literacy of a community even if they are not officially funded by a grant or a federal program. Funding for special programs for public libraries often come from the budget or from donations provided by the local friends group. Funding for school library programs may come from local businesses, service organizations, and donations from individuals. Chapter 7, "What Are the Steps to Preparing for a Family Literacy Event?," provides detailed options.

CONCLUSION

Who funds a literacy program for your library impacts the answers to five essential questions as posed in *Grants for Libraries* (Gerding & MacKellar, 2006, p. ix):

Does your library have the capacity to implement and support this project?
How will this grant make an impact?
Is your project sustainable?
Do you have real relationships with funders and partners?
How will you know that you've been successful?

Reference

Gerding, S. K., & MacKellar, P. H. (2006). *Grants for libraries: A how-to-do-it manual for librarians*. New York: Neal-Schuman.

CHAPTER 4

What Does Research Tell Us about Family Literacy?

Holly Weimar

Family literacy programs began to emerge in the 1980s (Griffis, 2003). With their emergence came legislation at the federal and state level that had a strong regulatory influence on many of the family literacy programs that were implemented. Depending on legislation and funding, family literacy programs have been regulated as to what elements should be included and evaluated. This has been the case with the Even Start programs throughout the United States. However, as some family literacy programs lose their funding, the program directors must look for new means for implementing the programs or they must abandon them. The results of this pattern are easily obtainable by conducting an Internet search for Even Start Family Literacy programs or other family literacy programs for individual states and checking the date associated with the Web page to see if it is static. Some of these sites will list that their funding has been lost.

With the loss of funding, family literacy programs that continue to survive do so with alternate influences. The most important influences, though, are those of the families that the programs serve. Researchers study family literacy programs, their components, and the results the programs have for those involved so that the public might learn more concerning the programs' effectiveness. Yet, each family literacy program is unique in its design and requires individual evaluation when attempting to assess the program. Learning about the design and the elements that make up a particular family literacy program to meet the needs of the children and the families involved will guide requests for future funding and how educators and organizations may contribute to future programs.

Once family literacy programs are understood as a whole, the decisions as to specific ways in which the school library should be involved may be made (Griffis, 2003). Every time that a family literacy program is implemented, it should strive to meet the needs of the unique families included to ensure the program's success. Meeting the needs of the families may incorporate many parameters. However, when families are successfully included in the design and implementation of the family literacy program, the results are higher completion rates of the families in the program, greater academic achievement for the children, improved behavior of the children in school, more parental involvement, and more favorable attitudes towards schooling.

PREMISE FOR RESEARCH

Much of the research begins with recognizing the following premise: a majority of the family literacy programs accept the principle that the parent is considered the child's first teacher (DeBruin-Parecki, 2009). With this being the case, DeBruin-Parecki (2009) recommends that parents establish good literacy habits themselves so they may assist their child.

Family literacy has its foundation set upon children and parents working with each other through family literacy programs. Heath (2010) points out that much of what is being asked of parents in family literacy programs is that they give to their child's education. However, it should be noted that when parents are requested to give to their child's education, this is not the same as participating with their child in learning experiences. The family literacy program should distinguish between the two perceptions for the parents. The program should enable the parents to grow in their knowledge of how to better participate in their child's learning experiences.

ADULT LITERACY

Educating the parents entails more than informing them about how to be a part of their child's educational experiences. One component of the family literacy program is increasing adult literacy. This component has important implications for the learning of children and adolescents (Lynch, 2009). Lynch's research brings together the relationship between the parents' educational levels and children's achievement, and the mother's literacy level and her child's literacy development. The first relationship establishes the link between parents' educational levels and children's achievement in school.

It has been shown that children whose parents have less than a high school education tend to have the poorest reading scores on standardized tests (Kogut, 2004). The higher the level of the parents' education, the better their children tend to do. The second relationship for children's literacy development and success is the mother's literacy level (U.S. Department of Education, 1999). The higher the literacy level of the mother, the better her child will perform. "Thus, effective adult literacy programs are not only important for adult literacy learning but are also important for the literacy development of children and adolescents" (Lynch, 2009, p. 509).

Adult literacy programs may have additional meaning for low-income mothers. Prins, Toso, and Schafft (2009) found that for women in poverty who had limited social support established supportive relationships and pursued self-development through the adult literacy portion of the family literacy program. For women who want the additional support, they may turn to the family literacy program to fulfill that need although men should not be ruled out as also needing or wanting this kind of support. The way in which family literacy programs allow adults to make connections with others is by "providing low income women and men with a space to encounter others in similar situations and, in turn, to discover, as one practitioner put it, 'that they're not alone in this world'" (Prins et al., 2009, p. 348). The key is having the time for adults to visit with one another in an informal setting where they may begin to make these connections. Time spent socializing with other participants might provide unanticipated positive outcomes for the women and men who might be seeking social support. These outcomes might include friendships, mentors, job references, and informal learning.

ATTENDANCE

While parents are included in family literacy programs, they may not always be regular attendees at the meetings. Educators should not jump to conclusions as to why they are not in attendance. Research has revealed that the belief that family literacy participants are unmotivated and may not sufficiently value education is still present among educators (Prins & Schafft, 2009). This belief may not be the truth. Each family should be viewed as unique, with their own set of needs. As to why a family may not participate or attend meetings and events on a regular basis requires inquiry. There may be underlying reasons that are not apparent to an educator who has not consulted the family about their lack of participation in the family literacy program.

For example, digital technology has "created a host of stressors that are challenging families" (Knopf & Swick, 2008, p. 420). Even though some parents may have the ability to work from home through the use of technology, these parents may have less time to spend with their children and their activities because of the increased amount of time they spend working. Knopf and Swick (2008) also point out that with more technology available, knowing how to use that technology may require parents to attend training, resulting in even more time away from the family. In addition, as technology infiltrates children's lives, children spend more time with technology and less time with parents (Knopf & Swick, 2008).

Prins and Schafft (2009) point to other stressors related to poverty and the conditions surrounding poverty that "make the pursuit of education, in many cases, a heroic endeavor" (p. 2302). These could be reasons as to why families are absent from family literacy programs. Other reasons might include not having work flexibility, extended family responsibilities, and other children (Staples & Diliberto, 2010). Even community conditions and government policies may inhibit family literacy participation (Prins & Schafft, 2009).

Single parenting may hinder parental involvement in family literacy programs as well. Single parents may have less time to participate because of the responsibilities placed upon them as sole provider for their children. Beyond the workday, the single parent must complete the meal routines and preparations for the next day for the family without help from another adult. Attempting to attend a family literacy event places additional responsibility on the single parent, especially if there is more than one child. By providing childcare and meals at the family literacy event, single parents might be encouraged to attend (Arnold, Zeljo, Doctoroff, & Ortiz, 2008; Timmons, 2008). It is important to note here that even two-parent homes may need accommodations such as these in order to stay involved (Knopf & Swick, 2008).

One group of parents and their children with whom family literacy designers should identify is immigrant English language learners (ELLs). Many of the ELLs who are of Latino origin make up the fastest growing population of learners in U.S. public schools (Iddings, 2009). Latino parents are supportive of literacy activities when they believe it will best help their child (Perry, Kay, & Brown, 2008). Yet, Latino parents will drop out of family literacy programs when the curriculum of the program goes against their child rearing or cultural beliefs (Janes & Kermani, 2001). However, when they do buy into the program, parents may modify literacy activities to reflect their cultural beliefs and practices (Perry et al., 2008). Once they integrate the literacy activities of the family literacy program into their shared learning experiences with their children, Latino parents may emphasize pleasure and enjoyment for motivational purposes, and use interaction, scaffolding, and the incorporation of moral messages (Perry et al., 2008).

While the population of the United States has changed and continues to do so, the family structure has changed, too. The family may no longer be thought of as mom and/or dad raising the children. "Multiplying patterns of living arrangements [mean] more and more children *stayed* more than they *lived* at certain addresses" (Heath, 2010. p. 29). These children may be carrying the burden of the conditions under which they live.

Heath (2010) notes that many children are affected by daily challenges such as illegal immigration, homelessness, and parents with addiction or mental health problems. When designing a family literacy program, knowing the families who will be involved will help with planning the activities and making other arrangements to meet their needs.

FAMILY LITERACY: ADOLESCENTS AND YOUNGER CHILDREN

When the family literacy program involves adolescents, special considerations might need to be made. Wiseman (2009) states "family support, relationships, and life contexts are different and unique" (p. 141) in regard to adolescents and their families. Recognizing this uniqueness when planning family literacy programs would be wise. One way to make sure that their needs are met would be to involve adolescent students when designing the program.

A misperception about adolescents is that they need less guidance and involvement with their families as they become more autonomous (Wiseman, 2009). In fact, adolescents desire the support of their parents though they may appear indifferent and may even challenge the support and structure that their parents provide (Cripps & Zyromski, 2009). A family literacy program with adolescent children and their parents could bridge the gap between home and school and provide support for the family while working towards boosting student achievement.

A word of caution: adolescents may affect their families' involvement in family literacy programs. Wiseman (2009) found that adolescents who felt that the family literacy program was harmonious with an activity that their parents would participate in would include them. Otherwise, they would not. Two reasons for adolescents not including parents were: (1) the personal nature of the content that might be revealed and (2) the perceived levels of stress and time constraints of their parents. To help overcome these obstacles, designers of family literacy programs need to listen to adolescents to know how to enhance their family literacy approach.

For younger children, parents who participate in family literacy programs may need specific suggestions for aiding their children with homework. They may also look for other ways of connecting with school literacy activities so that they may incorporate them into their daily lives with their children (Lynch, 2009). "Parents seek opportunities to have direct impacts on their children's education" (Knopf & Swick, 2008, p. 425).

Research has shown that by including literacy strategies and the vocabulary that goes along with it in the family literacy program, parents are better able to help their children. The parents who received this information through their program were able to list the strategies that they were taught and use the vocabulary involved in fluency instruction (Morrow, Mendelsohn, & Kuhn, 2010).

IMPACT OF PARENT INVOLVEMENT AND FAMILY LITERACY PROGRAMS

In addition, parents should be educated about the impact that their involvement in the school would have on the academic and personal development of their child (Cripps & Zyromski, 2009). Parent involvement has many benefits (Adams, Womack, Shatzer, & Caldarella, 2010). One benefit is the exchange of information between home and school. Also, parent involvement is associated with student academic achievement (Arnold et al., 2008; Desimone, 1999). Other benefits include improved behavior and attendance at a higher education institution. For prekindergarten children, parental involvement predicted higher levels of social skills and lower levels of problem behaviors (Powell, Son, File, & Juan, 2010). For the school, benefits include improved relationships with parents and greater support from parents.

The Latino population in the United States is growing. Latino parents should be actively involved in schools and attending family literacy programming. However, that may not always be what is happening. It really depends on the power structures within the school and those that govern the community. Latinos may not be highly represented within these organizational structures. As Latinos become more of a presence within these power structures, there will be an increase of Latino parents' involvement in the schools (Marschall, 2006). Encouraging Latino families to become active in the structures through the family literacy program may help increase participation in the program.

One school found a way to involve newly arrived immigrant families. Iddings (2009) describes The Welcome Center project that created a space within a school for these families to share with educators. The space allowed for family members to use resources and share their experiences. The educators learned from the families creating better understanding between home and school to support literacy. The benefits included gains in academic achievement for students, improved behavior in school, more favorable attitudes toward school, and enhanced English-language skills.

Just as The Welcome Center provided a place for resources and sharing for newly arrived immigrant families, perhaps all families might benefit from such a space. Barbarin and Aikens (2009) suggest that an optimal setting for promoting parental involvement includes the parents in "active participation either through discussion or learning activities" (p. 392). By tying a social purpose to this setting, the opportunity might present itself as more attractive; and, if the other elements of family literacy are included, a program is soon developed.

A word of caution about following the family literacy model: a problem lies with its orientation in that "it ignores, or in many cases disregards, the diverse childrearing practices that many families daily utilize to transmit certain values to their children and overlooks specific beliefs about childrearing—around issues such as discipline, feeding, and literacy development" (Johnson, 2009, p. 258). By valuing the knowledge that families possess and allowing families to be resources who share their experiences and ideas within the program, a family literacy program may grow richer.

TRANSNATIONAL LITERACY

Other opportunities for literacy development might be present in a program such as The Welcome Center. For families who have ties in other countries, they have the prospect to remain in contact with the family and friends they left behind. Jiménez, Smith, and Teague (2009) recommend incorporating transnational literacy into the program. Transnational literacy is a term that refers "to the written language practices of people who are involved in activities that span national boundaries" (p. 17). With the availability of digital technology, it is easy for families to remain in close contact with family and friends who live across national borders.

ORGANIZATIONAL SUPPORT FOR RESEARCH ON FAMILY LITERACY

Family literacy programs are envisioned as bringing together resources that will help parents and children with their literacy growth. "By purchasing print materials, taking pleasure in reading themselves, and encouraging children's use of books, parents transmit the value they attach to literacy" (Barbarin & Aikens, 2009, p. 384). The topic of family literacy was deemed important enough that the American Library Association (ALA) president-elect adopted it as part of her platform. At the 2009 ALA Annual Conference Meeting in Chicago, Camila Alire (2009), ALA's president-elect, announced her initiative for a family literacy focus to develop innovative family literacy models that would be replicable. What this means for libraries is that they would have family literacy programs that had proved successful and replicable made available to them in the near future. During the ALA conference, several family literacy programs were highlighted to begin the discussion and search.

An example of a family literacy program that is replicable and has proven successful is Prime Time. After a 10-year study, the program demonstrated a 76% retention rate and 120% attendance growth rate from session one to session eight (Barr, 2010, p. 2). The program may be found in 38 states where families with children who are in first through fourth grades may participate. The children who took part in the program outperformed children who were in the control group on grade-level assessments in all areas including reading, mathematics, and science (Barr, 2010).

Another organization that has an area in which literacy is of great interest is the American Educational Research Association (AERA). AERA may have American in its name but it is prominent internationally. The primary goal of AERA is to advance educational research and its practical application (AERA, 2011). Publications concerning educational research may be accessed from the association's website. In addition, AERA has a relatively new special interest group for school librarians called

Research, Education, Information, and School Libraries (REISL). When REISL and its promotion of school library research are combined with other areas of educational research, a rich environment of support develops for collaboration and student achievement. For those interested in sharing the results of their research concerning family literacy programs and school libraries, REISL is a forum for presenting and sharing information.

BUILDING BLOCKS OF FAMILY LITERACY FOR PARENT-CHILD INTERACTIONS

One of AERA's publications includes *Research Points*, which contains suggestions for policymakers (AERA, 2009). This publication reports that several decades of cumulative research shows that when beginning to read, skilled readers of English need to master several foundational building blocks for early literacy success. The first building block of early literacy contains the knowledge of phonological structures, alphabetic principles (how written symbols connect to spoken words), and fluency in decoding. A second building block is the development of oral language skills in young children. A third foundational building block is having children read. The time spent reading by children should be to improve their ability, vocabulary, and fluency. Children should read daily, and they should read increasingly challenging materials. It is purported that children will become skilled readers of English through the mastery of foundational literacy blocks.

However, not all family literacy programs include these foundational building blocks for early literacy. Some family literacy programs focus mainly on promoting shared reading between the parent and child as a way to increase literacy. Johnson, Martin, Brooks-Gunn, and Petrill (2008) found that it might be possible to improve literacy among young children using more than shared reading. They suggest that making books available in the home and encouraging the child to engage with books may be an effective approach to improving early literacy (p. 466). Interactive shared reading where children become engaged with the text has a greater effect on vocabulary than shared reading experiences with low levels of participation (Shanahan & Lonigan, 2010). Through engagement, the child will more than likely strengthen the skills he or she needs for school.

Helping parents to know what their children are learning and are expected to learn in school could increase the parent-child interactions during shared reading and increase the child's engagement with books. A family literacy program that supports parental involvement in a child's literacy includes a component where parents are taught strategies to help their child predict, respond to texts, explain, and elaborate upon texts (Paratore, Krol-Sinclair, David, & Schick, 2010). Parents would also learn to engage their child in discussing the text along with their own experiences. One of the goals would be to connect families to school by helping parents adopt the language used in classroom literacy instruction. Knowledge of language such as graphic organizers, reading response, and other terms enable parents to talk with their children and the teachers about the child's learning and the school's curriculum (Paratore et al., 2010).

Parents want to be participants in preparing their children for school. Barbarin and Aikens (2009) state parents' values and beliefs now favor academic (school) readiness, but they have yet to include the importance of higher-order thinking skills in their description of academic readiness. Barbarin and Aikens (2009) also note that parents' values and beliefs are more likely to influence the skills that their children acquire. This speaks volumes to including parents of young children who need help in this area in a family literacy program. The program would help parents learn the importance of higher-order thinking skills for their children's academic success.

What's more, Barbarin and Aikens (2009) describe the social context of parental practices as including "widely held beliefs about what children should learn prior to school entry and who is responsible for teaching these skills" (p. 386). Again, here is a place where family literacy programs can bridge the gap between home and school to help parents understand what their children will learn in the school environment. Through the program, families could gain knowledge about the school's curriculum and have access to resources to help them.

Through family literacy programs, parents could learn how other family members might be of support. For example, siblings could encourage and engage younger children with their literacy skills. If grandparents are available, they could participate in literacy activities as well. Different family members may play important roles in family literacy in transmitting reading and writing skills to children (Mui & Anderson, 2008).

If one family member is not helpful with literacy activities, then another may take his or her place. Martin, Ryan, and Brooks-Gunn (2010) found that fathers' supportiveness matters when a mother has low supportiveness for her children. In addition, fathers were especially important for predicting children's social competence. Yet, mothers still play an important role in the child's academic competence even when fathers were supportive. Grandparents and other adults significant in a child's life may also fill the gap when neither parent is supportive of their child.

How families organize themselves can vary among the different environments and cultural groups to which they belong. Mui and Anderson (2008) point out that "recently, educators have begun to realize that literacy is . . . composed of complex cultural and social practices that vary from context to context" (p. 234). Including family experiences in the family literacy program will make the differences of each family shared and known allowing for a richer experience for all of the families. In addition, the knowledge will inform educators who work with the children so that they are better able to meet their needs.

In areas where poverty is a factor, family literacy programs may provide help for families. Lynch (2009) recommends that educators study and explore the out-of-school literacy activities of low-income parents in order to better support their adult literacy learning, especially those who are from low-income backgrounds. One of the recommendations is to use everyday authentic general-use reading materials with parents (materials related to their child's schooling) to promote literacy. Another is to build upon previous experiences that were meaningful to the parents to increase their literacy learning.

For low-income children, family literacy programs have been established to offer support. During the summer, when children are out of school, low-income children have been identified as being at risk for falling behind in reading. Summer reading programs encourage children to read during the summer months. However, these programs do not guarantee success.

Kim and Guryan (2010) studied the effects of a voluntary summer reading program for fourth grade low-income Latino children with a family literacy component and found that there was no significant effect on reading comprehension and vocabulary. What this means is that in a summer reading program where the child was able to self-select books for reading and parents received training, as this program did, there is no guarantee that the child will make significant achievement in the areas of reading comprehension and vocabulary.

It is generally understood that during the summer months, when many children are out of the classroom, the opportunity for children to have access to a library and books comes from their family. The challenge becomes building a better family literacy summer reading program. Kim and Guryan (2010) use Chall's (1983) stage theory of reading where fourth grade children and above are identified as being more likely than younger children to be able to read independently without assistance because they have developed strong decoding skills. In addition, Kim and Guryan point out the importance of matching the child with the right book for reader ability and readability of texts. The Lexile framework, a leveled reading system by MetaMetrics, is recommended to help accomplish the match of a book to a child's independent reading level.

Prior to the end of the regular school year, teachers should begin scaffolding their students' voluntary reading by "encouraging children to read aloud with their parents, instructing children to use multiple strategies for comprehending text and releasing responsibility to children for practicing these strategies while reading books at home" (Kim & Guryan, 2010, p. 21). In addition, Kim and Guryan suggest that the summer reading program involve both parents and children and include teacher-directed vocabulary and comprehension lessons.

RESEARCH AND EVALUATION OF FAMILY LITERACY PROGRAMS

Lonigan and Shanahan (2010) discuss the importance of selecting programs for use when expecting results in increased development of early literacy skills. They researched programs that are professed to deliver these increases, but the research behind the programs may not necessarily show evidence of success in the way the programs are presented. When studying a family literacy program, it may be difficult to put in place the necessary experimental design for scientific study. Thus, many programs rely on qualitative methods to evaluate the program by using interviews, surveys, and other such narrative data, which may be useful only for that single group and should be conducted to tell the outcomes of the participants.

The types of assessment for family literacy programs may include several measures that look for program success. For example, one program assessed student achievement using mixed methods, which included both quantitative and qualitative measures (Morrow, Mendelsohn, & Kuhn, 2010). The quantitative measures included standardized test scores for reading. The qualitative measures were interviews with the children, parents, and teachers who participated in the family literacy program.

When conducting an evaluation begin by defining the family literacy program. Timmons (2008, p. 96) notes that there are many definitions and approaches to improving family literacy. Along with the definition, some key questions should be answered:

- What is the focus of the family literacy program?
- How does the program impact those involved?
- Does the family literacy program engage the family or only espouse family-centered philosophies?
- If families are involved, are they actively involved in the program design and delivery?

If families are involved in the program's design and delivery, there is a greater likelihood of the program's success (Timmons, 2008).

Other elements and questions to consider when evaluating a family literacy program include those that are similar to what the Delaware Family Literacy Program Review Instrument (Delaware Department of Education, 2008) uses. The Delaware Department of Education developed this instrument in response to the mandate by the U.S. Department of Education that all recipients of grant monies should monitor the performance of grant activities. Other state departments of education have created similar instruments for their programs. The elements included in the Delaware Family Literacy Program Review Instrument contain the following:

- A review of the administration and management of the program
- The instructional delivery process and procedures
- An examination of the qualification of the staff
- Availability of opportunities for staff development
- Support and assistance provided for students
- Collaborations with community partners
- A review of the facilities that includes the equipment as well as the location and the meeting rooms

Funding plays an important role in determining the design and length of a family literacy program. Due to lack of funding, a family literacy program may be limited in scope. When evaluating the family literacy program, the funding source, amount of funding, and limitations due to funding should be identified. On the brighter side, if funding should allow for a greater scope or duration of a family literacy program, this should be noted and broadcasted as a benefit with which the program is starting out to encourage greater participation, knowledge about the program, and the program's sustainability.

During the evaluation of the family literacy program, evidence of areas of difficulty may appear. Challenges to implementing the family literacy program should be noted. By recording the problems that are encountered and how they are handled, knowledge about how to avoid or work around the potential problem in the future may be acquired. No one wants to continually repeat mistakes because doing so could discourage families from wanting to be a part of the program. The goal of the program should be to support families in their participation.

Timmons (2008) encourages the use of authentic participation when developing a family literacy program. Timmons writes, "Because true family participation is a difficult and time-consuming process, it is much easier for organizations to deliver a packaged program than it is to work with families by looking at their needs and then creating and/or modifying a program so that it directly relates to them" (p. 98). By having families involved in the dialogue when developing the family literacy program, there will be a much greater probability that family needs will be heard and incorporated into the program.

Knowing how many families participate and who they are is done by keeping track of attendance. This is important for several reasons. First, the number of participants in the program will be needed for evaluation of effort. Second, attendance will provide knowledge of absenteeism. The latter reason proves useful if the family literacy program is accumulative with each session building upon the last. If absenteeism is high, this could produce problems for successive meetings, with families beginning to feel frustrated, lost, or disconnected (Timmons, 2008). In addition, the dropout rate for families will need to be known.

Another important area for assessment of the family literacy program is in the area of diversity. It should be evaluated for how it meets the needs of diverse populations. Timmons (2008) reports that culturally responsive educators who respect and incorporate cultural aspects from the families who are participating in the family literacy program will experience a higher retention rate, academic achievement, and parental involvement in the school.

To formally evaluate the family literacy program, Timmons (2008) recommends looking at the age of the children and the type of family literacy program in which they are involved. A pretest/posttest assessment may be used to see the gains the children made. For scientific research, a control group will need to be in place. To establish the control group and avoid ethical challenges, Timmons suggests that half of the children who sign up for the family literacy program be randomly assigned to the control group in the fall while the others are assigned to the family literacy program. When spring comes around, the control group may then be served by the family literacy program.

The New Jersey State Department of Education (2010) has a website with a checklist for evaluating family literacy programs. More items than are included in the following list should be in the program's checklist. The checklist could contain information previously discussed. Items that are included in the New Jersey State Department of Education checklist are the following:

- Demographic information for informing program funders and identifying possible needs
- Identification of personal educational goals, family and parenting goals—including what parents want to do with children (Tice, 2000)

Prins, Toso, and Schafft (2009) lament that "conventional program evaluation methods and federal and state accountability measures seldom recognize the social functions" of family literacy programming (p. 349). This might be because the evaluation methods are based more on scientific measures looking for academic gains rather than on qualitative methods where interviews may be conducted and stories shared by the participants. Personal interviews, simple surveys that allow participants to answer some open-ended questions, and case studies will allow researchers to gather data about how participants function socially within the program.

SOME LONG-TERM RESULTS OF FAMILY LITERACY

Some family literacy programs have been in practice long enough for data to be collected on students who are of age to have enrolled in institutions of higher education. What are some of the long-term effects? Paratore, Krol-Sinclair, David, and Schick (2010) conducted research to find out. When they compared the family literacy participants to the general student population, the family literacy students demonstrated the following:

- Higher rates of school attendance
- GPA that exceeded that of the general school population
- Better scores on the English language arts and mathematics state assessments in grades 4, 8, and 10
- 80% completion rate for school

These results are briefly described here for the purpose of demonstrating the long-term effects family literacy programs may have.

CONCLUSION

Each family literacy program is unique in its design and in its attempt to strive to meet the needs of the participating families to ensure the program's success. When designing and implementing the family literacy program, families should be included in the planning in order to obtain the results of higher completion rates for the families in the program, greater academic achievement for the children, improved behavior of the children in school, more parental involvement, and more favorable attitudes towards schooling. Although the individual programs are unique, they maintain common components, such as adult literacy, parental support for the children, opportunities and activities for parents and children to connect, and information for parents regarding the importance of their involvement in school and its association with student academic achievement and improved behavior.

In addition to the design and implementation of a family literacy programs, the evaluation of the program is important. When evaluating a family literacy program, components such as the process and procedures involved with instructional delivery and a review of the facilities are desired. While there are other considerations that may be tied to funding and research for evaluating family literacy programs, the goal is to have long-term effects for the success of children and their families.

References

Adams, M.B., Womack, S.A., Shatzer, R.H., & Caldarella, P. (2010). Parent involvement in school-wide social skills instruction: Perceptions of a home note program. *Education, 130*(3), 513–528.

Alire, C. (2009). President-elect report. *Proceedings of the 2009 ALA Annual Conference Meeting, Chicago.* Retrieved from http://www.ala.org/ala/aboutala/governance/council/cmte_info_report/2009annual_cmte_info_rpts/29_1_pres_elect.pdf

American Educational Research Association. (2011). *About AERA.* Retrieved from https://www.aera.net/AboutAERA.htm

American Educational Research Association. (2009). Ensuring early literacy success. *Research Points: Essential Information for Education Policy, 6*(1), 1–4.

Arnold, D. H., Zeljo, A., Doctoroff, G.L., & Ortiz, C. (2008). Parent involvement in preschool: Predictors and the relation of involvement to pre-literacy development. *School Psychology Review, 37*(1), 74–90.

Barbarin, O. A., & Aikens, N. (2009). Supporting parental practices in the language and literacy development of young children. In O.A. Barbarin & B.H. Wasik (Eds.), *Handbook of child development and early education: Research to practice* (pp. 378–398). New York: The Guilford Press.

Barr, J. E. (2010). *Stemming the tide of intergenerational illiteracy: A ten-year impact study of prime time family reading time* New Orleans: Louisiana Endowment for the Humanities. Retrieved from http://www.leh.org/primetime/pt10yrstudy.pdf

Chall, J. S. (1983). *Stages of reading development.* New York: McGraw-Hill.

Cripps, K., & Zyromski, B. (2009). Adolescents psychological well-being and perceived parental involvement: Implications for parental involvement in middle schools. *Research in Middle Level Education Online, 33*(4), 1–13.

DeBruin-Parecki, A. (2009). Establishing a family literacy program with a focus on interactive reading: The role of research and accountability. *Early Childhood Education Journal, 36*(5), 385–392.

Delaware Department of Education. (2008). *Guidelines for family literacy program review.* Retrieved from http://www.acenetwork.org/index.html

Desimone, L. (1999). Linking parent involvement with student achievement: Do race and income matter? *Journal of Educational Research, 93*(1), 11.

Griffis, J. (2003). Family literacy programs in school libraries: Helping parents become their child's best teacher. *Library Media Connection, 22*(1), 30–34.

Heath, S.B. (2010). Family literacy or community learning? Some critical questions on perspective. In K. Dunsmore & D. Fisher (Eds.), *Bringing literacy home* (pp. 15–41). Newark, DE: International Reading Association.

Iddings, A. (2009). Bridging home and school literacy practices: Empowering families of recent immigrant children. *Theory into Practice, 48*(4), 304–311.

Janes, H., & Kermani, H. (2001). Caregivers' story reading to young children in family literacy programs: Pleasure or punishment? *Journal of Adolescent & Adult Literacy, 44*(5), 455.

Jiménez, R., Smith, P., & Teague, B. (2009). Transnational and community literacies for teachers. *Journal of Adolescent & Adult Literacy, 53*(1), 16–26.

Johnson, A., Martin, A., Brooks-Gunn, J., & Petrill, S. (2008). Order in the house! Associations among household chaos, the home literacy environment, maternal reading ability, and children's early reading. *Merrill-Palmer Quarterly, 54*(4), 445–472.

Johnson, L. (2009). Challenging "best practices" in family literacy and parent education programs: The development and enactment of mothering knowledge among Puerto Rican and Latina mothers in Chicago. *Anthropology & Education Quarterly, 40*(3), 257–276.

Kim, J.S., & Guryan, J. (2010). The efficacy of a voluntary summer book reading intervention for low-income Latino children from language minority families. *Journal of Educational Psychology, 102*(1), 20–31.

Knopf, H., & Swick, K. (2008). Using our understanding of families to strengthen family involvement. *Early Childhood Education Journal, 35*(5), 419–427.

Kogut, B. (2004). Why adult literacy matters. *Phi Kappa Phi Forum, 84*(2), 26–28.

Lonigan, C.J., & Shanahan, T. (2010). Developing early literacy skills: Things we know we know and things we know we don't know. *Educational Researcher, 39*(4), 340–346.

Lynch, J. (2009). Print literacy engagement of parents from low-income backgrounds: Implications for adult and family literacy programs. *Journal of Adolescent & Adult Literacy, 52*(6), 509–521.

Marschall, M. (2006). Parent involvement and educational outcomes for Latino students. *Review of Policy Research, 23*(5), 1053–1076.

Martin, A., Ryan, R.M., & Brooks-Gunn, J. (2010). When fathers' supportiveness matters most: Maternal and paternal parenting and children's school readiness. *Journal of Family Psychology, 24*(2), 145–155.

Morrow, L.M., Mendelsohn, A.L., & Kuhn, M.R. (2010). Characteristics of three family literacy programs that worked. In K. Dunsmore & D. Fisher (Eds.), *Bringing literacy home* (pp. 83–103). Newark, DE: International Reading Association.

Mui, S., & Anderson, J. (2008). At home with the Johars: Another look at family literacy. *The Reading Teacher, 62*(3), 234–243.

New Jersey State Department of Education. (2010). *Even Start Family Literacy: Local program evaluation outline.* Retrieved from http://www.state.nj.us/education/titles/title1/even/eval.htm

Paratore, J. R., Krol-Sinclair, B., David, B., & Schick, A. (2010). Writing the next chapter in family literacy: Clues to long-term effects. In K. Dunsmore & D. Fisher (Eds.), *Bringing literacy home* (pp. 265–288). Newark, DE: International Reading Association.

Perry, N. J., Kay, S., & Brown, A. (2008). Continuity and change in home literacy practices of Hispanic families with preschool children. *Early Child Development & Care, 178*(1), 99–113.

Powell, D. R., Son, S., File, N., & Juan, R. R. S. (2010). Parent-school relationships and children's academic and social outcomes in public school pre-kindergarten. *Journal of School Psychology, 48*(4), 269–292.

Prins, E., & Schafft, K. A. (2009). Individual and structural attributions for poverty and persistence in family literacy programs: The resurgence of the culture of poverty. *Teachers College Record, 111*(9), 2280–2310.

Prins, E., Toso, B., & Schafft, K. (2009). "It feels like a little family to me": Social interaction and support among women in adult education and family literacy. *Adult Education Quarterly, 59*(4), 335–352.

Shanahan, T. & Lonigan, C. J. (2010). The National Early Literacy Panel: A summary of the process and the report. *Educational Researcher, 39*(279), 279–285.

Staples, K. E., & Diliberto, J. A. (2010). Guidelines for successful parent involvement. *Teaching Exceptional Children, 42*(6), 58–63.

Tice, C. J. (2000). Enhancing family literacy through collaboration: Program considerations. *Journal of Adolescent & Adult Literacy, 44*(2), 138.

Timmons, V. (2008). Challenges in researching family literacy programs. *Canadian Psychology, 49*(2), 96–102.

U.S. Department of Education. (1999). *America reads: Start early, finish strong.* Washington D.C.: Author.

Wiseman, A. (2009). "When you do your best, there's someone to encourage you": Adolescents' views of family literacy. *Journal of Adolescent & Adult Literacy, 53*(2), 132–142.

CHAPTER 5

What Does Research Tell Us about the Importance of Reading?

As stated in chapter 1, "literacy" traditionally means the ability to read and write, to recognize words, and to write words in a sentence. Understanding the importance of reading in relationship to family literacy becomes understanding the research into reading and especially the importance of reading related to children's academic achievement and to their basic success in life. Three champions of literacy come to mind: Stephen Krashen, Jim Trelease, and Keith Lance. Krashen and Trelease are long-time experts in the field of reading application. Lance brings his expertise in researching school library services and how they impact student achievement.

Krashen has recommended free voluntary reading as a method of encouraging reading experience and increasing a young person's reading skills. Much of his philosophy and research is explained and demonstrated in *The Power of Reading: Insights from the Research* (the second edition was published in 2004 by Libraries Unlimited) and in *Free Voluntary Reading*, a collection of his essays published by Libraries Unlimited in 2011.

Jim Trelease's classic, bestselling book, *The Read-Aloud Handbook* (2006), was first published in 1982 and continues to impact the lives of parents and their children, and teachers and the children they work with. Krashen and Trelease are champions of reading, books, and education. Their writings and books should be studied by school administrators, school and public librarians, reading teachers and professionals, and, especially, parents.

STEPHEN D. KRASHEN

Stephen D. Krashen is Emeritus Professor of Education at the University of Southern California. He is a linguist, an educational researcher, and an activist. His fields are second language acquisition, bilingual education, and reading. His books about reading and bilingual education include:

Every Person a Reader: An Alternative to the California Task Force Report on Reading (1996)
Explorations in Language Acquisition and Use (2003)
Free Voluntary Reading (2011)
The Power of Reading: Insights from the Research (2004)
Three Arguments against Whole Language and Why They Are Wrong (1999)

Krashen is a proponent of specific beliefs about readers from his years of reviewing educational research. He is passionate about the best ways for children to become readers. Those ideas and beliefs can be found in numerous letters to the editor, articles, and books, and in his presence on listservs and Twitter. Two of his major beliefs related to literacy that are most appropriate to family literacy in particular are free voluntary reading and the negative impact of poverty on children's reading and education.

Free Voluntary Reading

Krashen's idea of free voluntary reading (FVR) is "reading because you want to. For school-age children, FVR means no book report, no questions at the end of the chapter, and no looking up every vocabulary word. FVR means putting down a book you don't like and choosing another one instead. It is the kind of reading highly literate people do all the time" (2004, p. x).

Krashen continues: "I will not claim that FVR is the complete answer. Free readers are not guaranteed admission to Harvard Law School. What the research tells me is that when children or less literate adults start reading for pleasure, however, good things will happen. Their reading comprehension will improve, and they will find difficult, academic-style texts easier to read. Their writing style will improve, and they will be better able to write prose in a style that is acceptable to schools, business, and the scientific community. Their vocabulary will improve, and their spelling and control of grammar will improve" (2004, p. x).

Reading for pleasure, freely selecting books that appeal, being free to "dump" a book if it's unappealing, having access to librarians who know how to help children locate books they will enjoy (readers' advisory techniques), having time to read, and having quality, appealing books readily available to children add up to the foundation of a successful FVR program.

Krashen concludes from his review of research on reading that reading for pleasure is more efficient and more successful than direct instruction in reading. He maintains that "researchers in early reading development have concluded that we 'learn to read by reading'" (2004, p. 37). FVR can move children to higher levels of proficiency in spelling, comprehension, and vocabulary, and can help them become more proficient writers. A popular method of FVR that librarians and teachers in schools use is sustained silent reading (SSR). Other terms may be used for this method, such as DEAR (drop everything and read). Students in a classroom or in an entire school are given at least 20 minutes a week to read for pleasure. To make significant gains in reading, research shows that students must have at least 45 minutes a week to read independently. Success of SSR depends upon having a wide selection of books and magazines available in either the classroom or library or both. Students should be allowed to read magazines, comics, graphic novels, informational books, and fiction— any type of print material that is appropriate to their grade level. During school-wide SSR, teachers and librarians and other school personnel should also be reading for pleasure to model this activity for students.

Krashen's findings and conclusions from research may seem too obvious and too good to be true, but reading well takes practice, just as learning to swim or ride a bike well takes practice. FVR is not a panacea for reading problems, but when consistently allowed and encouraged in schools, it can make an impressive impact on improving students' reading ability. The following are gems about reading from *The Power of Reading*:

> The more access children have to books at home, at school, or at the public library, the more they read. (p. 58)
>
> Larger school library collections and longer hours increase circulation, as do more organized visits to the library. (p. 59)
>
> Library quality (books and staffing) is related to reading achievement. (p. 66)
>
> Children from high-income families are "deluged" with books; children from low-income families must "aggressively and persistently seek them out." (p. 68)
>
> Reading itself promotes reading. (p. 81)
>
> Sometimes one positive reading experience can create a reader. (p. 82)
>
> Children read more when they have time to read. (p. 85)
>
> Light reading is the way nearly all of us learned to read. (p. 92) (Comics, short book series, and magazines are considered light reading.)
>
> Light reading isn't enough, but it can lead to heavier reading. (p. 116)
>
> Rewarding reading sends the message that reading is unpleasant or not worth doing without a reward. (p. 117)

Readers who can "get lost in a book" have the best chance of becoming excellent readers. When readers get lost in a book, they find such pleasure in a story or in a book's information that they become totally absorbed in the experience. Individual readers will each have their own special interests. For some that means mysteries or baseball stories or information about volcanoes. Recent popular books that children and teens voted as their favorites can be found through the International Reading Association's Children's Choices lists (http://www.reading.org/Resources/Booklists/ChildrensChoices.aspx) and Young Adult's Choices lists (http://www.reading.org/Resources/Booklists/YoungAdultsChoices.aspx). When looking for popular reading selections, these two annual lists are a great place to start.

Impact of Poverty on Literacy

As an education and reading activist, Krashen's current battle cry targets poverty as the culprit for low reading scores, not teachers, parents, and our education system. Researchers have targeted poverty before now as a reason for lack of success in school. Krashen and others go one step further and make recommendations for what schools can do and what they are doing that works. School systems can:

1. Continue and expand free and reduced meal programs.
2. Continue applying for literacy grants to fund libraries, training of teachers, and consistent literacy sessions for parents and children.
3. Increase the number of school nurses in schools, especially in poverty areas where health insurance may be lacking.
4. Increase funding for school library book collections and classroom book collections to help students who have few or no books at home.
5. Provide access to school libraries for students and their parents in late afternoons, evenings, and on Saturdays.

Krashen maintains that eliminating most standardized tests and redirecting the cost of testing will pay for the expense of more school nurses and better school libraries. Based on his reviews of research about education and reading in the United States and internationally, attacking poverty and promoting free voluntary reading will greatly improve literacy, increasing reading scores and academic success in schools (Morrow, 1983).

JIM TRELEASE

Jim Trelease is known for his read-aloud handbook that he self-published in 1979. *The Read-Aloud Handbook* is now in its sixth edition and has been published in Britain, Australia, Spain, China, and Japan. Trelease was not a reading expert; he was a writer and an artist working for a daily newspaper in Massachusetts. Perhaps most importantly, he was a parent of two sons with whom he shared his love of stories and books. As a result of this connection with his children and with books, he wrote a pamphlet about reading aloud to children, and it was published a few years later by Penguin Books. From 1983 until his retirement, Trelease has worked full-time as a lecturer and advocate of the benefits of reading aloud to children. A dynamic speaker and a master of reading aloud, Trelease has entertained and inspired teachers, librarians, and parents with his enthusiasm and knowledge. After 25 years, Trelease has discontinued public speaking but maintains an active and useful Web page at http://www.trelease-on-reading.com.

The Read-Aloud Handbook addresses three major areas: reading aloud, topics related to reading, and a treasury of recommended titles. The sixth and latest edition continues to answer basic questions about reading aloud:

1. Why should we read aloud to children?
2. When should we begin reading aloud?
3. What are the stages of reading aloud?
4. What are the dos and don'ts of reading aloud?
5. What can sustained silent reading (SSR) do for students?

The sixth edition incorporates Trelease's experiences, philosophy, and relevant research about reading aloud and related issues. The newest edition ends with four chapters: "In Their Own Words"; "The Print Climate in the Home, School, and Library"; "Lessons from Oprah, Harry, and the Internet"; and "TV, Audio, and Technology: Hurting or Helping Literacy?" The last major section of the book is the treasury of read-alouds. The treasury is divided into wordless books, predictable books, reference books, picture books, short novels, full-length novels, poetry, anthologies, and fairy and folk tales. Each selection includes a description of the book, recommended listening grade levels, and a brief list of related books. Of course each title is recommended by Trelease, and he has included old and new titles and titles that were in print at the time of publication of this starter list of read-alouds.

Reading Research Statistics

Trelease incorporates a wide variety of research studies that are directed at demonstrating how books and reading in the home can make a huge difference in the lives of children as they progress through adulthood. Sources, more details of the studies, and Trelease's comments are found in the sixth edition of *The Read-Aloud Handbook*. A handful of studies are briefly described below but many more are available in the sixth edition.

1. Reading interests of mothers and fathers impact children's interest in books, either negatively or positively. In the *Journal of Educational Research*, a 1983 study showed that kindergartners who had a high interest in books had mothers and fathers who read avidly. There were books in the home, and children owned library cards, were taken to the library, and were read to daily.

2. Kindergartners begin school eager to learn to read. According to the National Reading Report Card, children's enthusiasm declines as they grow older. By the 4th grade, only 54% are reading for pleasure every day. By 8th grade, only 30% are reading for pleasure every day. By 12th grade, only 19% are reading for pleasure every day.

3. In a study published in 1996 and entitled *Meaningful Differences in the Everyday Experience of Young American Children*, researchers reported about words that children heard from age seven months to age four years. In the 42 families studied, four-year-olds in professional families heard 45 million words; children in working-class families heard 26 million; and children in welfare families heard only 13 million. Trelease points out that it is impossible for teachers to make up this word gap in the classroom.

Advice about Nurturing Readers

Throughout *The Read-Aloud Handbook* Trelease intermingles his advice with his review of research about reading. From his own experience as a reader, as a parent, and from hearing about other people's reading experiences, he offers realistic advice for educators, librarians, parents, and caregivers who want children to become strong, skillful readers. These bits of advice are based on Trelease's extended explanations and are basic advice. He gives more detailed advice about book selection, reading aloud, and sustained silent reading than can be shared here.

Basic Advice for Parents

1. Speak to children in meaningful ways as soon as they are born. They need the conditioning of hearing language from their parents.
2. Read to children as soon as they are born. They need to hear a variety of vocabulary and the structure of language from books.
3. Read one-to-one with your child for expanding his or her reading attention.
4. Read to children as often as possible, showing your pleasure in a story.
5. Read the same books repeatedly if the child wants to hear them again and again.
6. Let children see you reading for pleasure.
7. Share with your children why you enjoy reading and books.
8. Buy books for your children or take them to the public library to choose their own books.
9. Allow children to quit a book if they don't like it.

10. Continue reading aloud to your children even after they have learned to read and even when they're teenagers.
11. Read books your children and teens are reading so you can share the experience.

Basic Advice for Teachers and Librarians

1. Read aloud to your students every day.
2. Observe SSR in your classroom at least 45 minutes every week.
3. Maintain a classroom collection of a variety of books and magazines.
4. Take your students to the school library as often as possible.
5. Let students see you reading for pleasure.
6. Learn what your students like to read, and read as many of those selections as you can.
7. Booktalk a variety of selections you think your students will enjoy.
8. Discuss stories with students after you have read them aloud.
9. Beware of computerized book programs that narrow readers' selections and tempt students with points.
10. Make the library "user-friendly."
11. Study successful marketing in bookstores. Include as much shelf space as you can that shows title pages (face-out shelving).

KEITH LANCE

Keith Lance is the founder and long-time director of the Library Research Service of the Colorado State Library and the University of Denver. His initial groundbreaking study of the impact of school library media programs on the academic achievement of U.S. public school students has been replicated in other states besides Colorado with consistent results. Evidence of the studies described in Lance's 2001 article "The Proof of the Power" demonstrates the value of:

1. Quality collections of books and other materials selected to support the curriculum.
2. State-of-the-art technology that is integrated into the learning/teaching processes.
3. Cooperation between school and other types of libraries, especially public libraries. (p. 14)

Most relevant to the topic of reading research is the confirmation that quality book and other materials collections make a positive impact on student achievement. This evidence reinforces the conclusions drawn by Krashen and Trelease that young people must have a large and varied collection available to them if they are to develop significantly as readers. For further information about this research visit Lance's Web page at http://www.keithcurrylance.com.

CONCLUSION

Stephen Krashen and Jim Trelease have stayed true to their conclusions about reading and education from reviewing research and from their own experiences that allowing and encouraging students to read for pleasure will strengthen their reading and writing abilities and that poverty is a huge barrier to literacy and to student achievement. All three men, including Keith Lance, recognize the need for emerging readers to be surrounded by print materials, and they are advocates for public and school libraries and for librarians as necessary to produce successful readers.

References

Krashen, S. D. (2004). *The power of reading: Insights from the research* (2nd ed.). Westport, CT: Libraries Unlimited.

Lance, K. (2001). Proof of the power: Quality library media programs affect academic achievement. *Multimedia Schools, 8*(4), 14.

Trelease, J. (2006). *The read-aloud handbook* (6th ed.). New York: Penguin.

CHAPTER 6

What Is a Family Literacy Event?

When thinking about the roots of children's literacy development, the family structure often comes to mind. We tell parents they are their child's first teacher. In many situations, family literacy occurs naturally as parents go about their daily routine and interact with their children. For example, parents and children often interact through making and using grocery shopping lists, following map directions, and sharing nightly storytimes. In many families, these are naturally occurring events with little pre-thought or planning. These are often the children we talk about as coming to prekindergarten or kindergarten ready to learn. They have received the foundation of language and literacy at home, and their parents have often taken them to the public library for storytimes and other reading readiness programs. They are ready for more formal instruction in an education setting.

In other families, these kinds of natural interactions are rare. No books are in the home. No one is available to take them to the public library, and they often do not go to prekindergarten. When children in these families enter our schools, we often say they are not ready for learning and have limited language or literacy experiences. These are often the children we later describe as academically at risk for school failure. Different states have different definitions of "at risk." However, No Child Left Behind (NCLB, 2001) summarizes at-risk students as children who are in

47

minority groups, are poor, have disabilities, or who speak a language other than English (NCLB, 2001).

For families with children who fit any or all of these at risk descriptors, family literacy programs can be viewed as intervention or support to develop family members' literacy skills. Family literacy has the potential to make a difference in a child's and family's life. According to Wasik (2004), the basic tenet of family literacy programs is "the intergenerational transmission of literacy from one family member to another" (p. 619). Literacy transmission between generations can be accomplished by using family adults to demonstrate, model, and guide children in literacy-related activities. Different library programs offering a variety of activities can help promote family literacy.

FEDERAL GOVERNMENT'S DEFINITION OF COMPREHENSIVE PROGRAM

A variety of models can help you plan for your family literacy program. A comprehensive family literacy program would address all family members from infant to grandparents and possibly extended family members who live in the home. According to Wasik (2004), these comprehensive programs would include four sections: early childhood education, adult education, parenting education and support, and parent-child literacy interactions. However, many entities are not set up to support all of the components. For example, due to personnel limitations, many schools are exceptionally qualified to address children's language and literacy needs, but have no one qualified to address adult education. If adult education is a goal for the school, then partnerships with outside agencies will be vital.

NATIONAL MODEL PROGRAMS

Among the national family literacy program models, Kentucky's Parent and Child Education Program (PACE) is often considered the original model to follow when planning a family literacy program. The PACE program targets families who have at least one child between three and four years old and in which one or both parents are without a high school diploma or equivalency. This was the first known program to serve two generations in tandem. Their overall goal was to help break the "strong, intergenerational cycle of undereducation and poverty" (University of Kentucky Appalachian Center, 2010). The specifics of the program can still be found interlaced in many newer programs today.

The program particulars described in the original research brief (Townley, Heberle, & Kim, 1988) include:

1. Raise the educational level of the parents of preschool children through instruction in basic skills.
2. Enhance parenting skills.
3. Increase developmental skills of preschool children to better prepare them for academic success.
4. Enable parents to become familiar with and comfortable in the school setting.
5. Provide a role model for the child that demonstrates parental interest in education.
6. Enhance the relationship of the parent and child through planned, structured interaction.
7. Demonstrate to parents their power to affect their child's ability to learn.
8. Encourage early identification and treatment of physical or mental handicaps that may inhibit children's learning ability.
9. Encourage identification and treatment of any handicapping conditions in the adult that may inhibit their ability to care for their children.

One of the more widely recognized family literacy models is the federal government's Even Start Family Literacy Program, commonly referred to as Even Start (RMC Research Corporation, 2001). Participants must meet certain requirements. One adult must be eligible for adult education services as described by the Adult Education Act and have one or more children under the age of eight. The program takes place at a center and can be supplemented with home visits.

The federal government provides funds to state level education agencies, who then distribute funds to their local education agencies through a competitive process. Even Start encompasses all four areas of a comprehensive family literacy program (early childhood education, adult education, parenting education and support, and parent-child literacy interactions). The early childhood component provides literacy instruction to children in a preschool program or in a home environment. The adult education piece creates opportunities for adults to earn their high school diploma, learn job skills, or improve their literacy skills. Parent education offers parenting classes concerning such topics as child development and parent support groups. Parent-child literacy interactions allow for regularly scheduled events when parents and children interact with the leader who guides children's language and literacy development.

The University of Illinois at Chicago's Project FLAME is a family literacy program serving Hispanic families across the United States (Project FLAME, 2003). It originated in the Chicago area and has spread to nine states and British Columbia. FLAME stands for Family Literacy: Aprendiendo, Mejorando, Educando. This can be translated as Family Literacy: Learning, Improving, Educating. Project FLAME's (2003) objectives are: "The 2–8 year old children of limited English proficient (LEP) parents will realize improved achievement in school, particularly in reading and writing tasks as a result of their parents' knowledge about literacy and enhanced opportunities for learning at home. LEP parents will have greater confidence in their ability to share their literacy with their children. LEP parents will increase their literacy knowledge and acquire strategies to provide literacy opportunities at home. LEP parents will improve their own literacy in both native language and English."

FLAME bases its activities on four dimensions of literacy learning. FLAME's belief about "Literacy Opportunity" believes access to childrens' books in the home is essential. The idea of "Literacy Modeling" indicates children need an adult model so they can imitate their reading behaviors. "Literacy Interaction" refers to any intentional exchange between parents and their children to enhance the children's literacy. "Home School Relations" ensures parents understand what the school is trying to accomplish and that teachers need to understand the parents' concerns.

This program is centered on three components: literacy lessons, English as a Second Language (ESL) classes, and community workshops. Twelve family literacy sessions include lessons about such things as book sharing, using the library, teaching the ABC's, creating home literacy centers, parent-teacher get-togethers, and songs, games, and language. ESL classes are held two days a week for the parents. Three days a year, parents and FLAME leaders attend workshops to educate families about community information and resources such as immigration laws and gang awareness.

Another popular program is Prime Time Family Reading Time developed by the Louisiana Endowment of the Humanities (n.d.) in cooperation with the National Endowment for the Humanities. This program was created with grant monies and has spread to 1,000 sites in 38 states. Their mission statement asserts: "In light of statewide needs, the mission of PRIME TIME FAMILY READING TIME® is to support inter-generational literacy and offer opportunities for rigorous, thought-provoking, value-centered humanities experiences for children and their families." Prime Time serves to bring children and adults together for a family story time hosted by great storytellers who use award-winning picture books. Although the stories concern diverse cultures, the audience is brought together in an open discussion around a humanities-related theme like honesty or pride. A person skilled in the area of humanities guides discussions to get parents and children talking about the theme revealed in the book and expertly tie it back in to the real lives of the families in attendance. Prime Time addresses only one of the four components previously described by Wasik (2004) as a comprehensive program. The six- to eight-week program can be implemented in many settings, such as public libraries and schools.

The National Center for Family Literacy (NCFL) was established in 1989 to assist families across America learn and grow together (National Center for Family Literacy, 2011). They have worked through community partners to develop model programs. One of their models is the Toyota Family Literacy Program, which serves families with elementary-aged children with ESL. This program addresses two of the four components as defined by the federal government. They address adult literacy skills and work to increase parental involvement in their children's education.

Another NCFL model program addresses the needs of American Indian families with children from birth through third grade. The Family and Child Education program is sustained by the Bureau of Indian Education. Their goal is to provide culturally responsive education, resources, and support to American Indian parents and children. They work in both the school and home environment to cover the three components of early childhood education, parenting education and support, and parent-child literacy interactions.

AT YOUR LIBRARY

Many of the above models offer a curriculum you can purchase or offer you the opportunity to join on a national level. However, for many of you, it will be important to get started with a minimal budget and minimal upfront support. In those cases, you could simply begin by hosting a family literacy night at your public library or assist with a program at the school library. This will help you get your feet wet and give you experience in this area. You can ascertain what aspects worked and what areas need further thought.

Looking back at the four components of a model program, you could simply focus on parent-child literacy interactions. Because story time is a regular event in most public libraries, this interaction could be hosting a family story time followed by a craft project or a simple theme-related snack. If this interaction is to be held in the school, one of the lower elementary grade teachers could help you plan this type of event. This kind of story time would resemble a fun, class lesson conducted with a much larger audience.

Public libraries often have limited space available for many groups, but school librarians may host multiple story rooms aimed at different ages or different interests. Do you have access to a local celebrity, a local politician, school board member, or news personality? Finding a guest story time reader well known by your audience can help draw a crowd. Think outside the box and consider renting a character costume from a popular children's book. What pre-K, kindergarten, first, or second grader would choose to miss out on a visit by Clifford the Big Red Dog or the Cat in the Hat?

Because public librarians often have access to community resources such as an adult literacy organization that often hosts adult literacy classes, you could bridge the relationship between your parents and families to adult education offered by the public library or another community resource. Depending on the policies of the community group, you could distribute flyers announcing their events and services, arrange transportation to their site, or offer a meeting place at your library or school.

Many schools have a parent liaison or parent facilitators located on their campus. If you can share with your school librarian for this kind of support contact, consider working with them to offer training to your parents who have young children not yet in school at the public library or at the school. The Houston Children's Museum has developed a program titled Para Los Niño's (Children's Museum of Houston, 2010). The program is housed online and is available to download for free. It was developed to use with parents whose primary language is Spanish and have preschool-age children. While it does mention a focus on Spanish-speaking families, the lessons work well with all families. These units are preplanned with step-by-step instructions to guide the leader through a story time and planned activities. The toolkit on their website has a list of all needed materials.

CONCLUSION

The following chapter will help you develop a plan to successfully implement a fantastic event for your students and families. You will discover more details related to personnel needed, both professional and volunteers, and steps to help you plan and prepare.

References

Children's Museum of Houston. (2010). *Para los niños—family learning programs for Spanish speaking parents*. Retrieved from http://www.cmhouston.org/losninos/.

Louisiana Endowment for the Humanities. (n.d.). *Prime time family reading time*. Retrieved from http://www.leh.org/html/primetime.html.

National Center for Family Literacy. (2011). *National center for family literacy*. Retrieved from http://www.famlit.org/.

No Child Left Behind Act of 2001. Public Law 107–110 (January 8, 2002).

Project FLAME. (2003). *Project FLAME university of Illinois at Chicago*. Retrieved from http://www.uic.edu/educ/flame/.

RMC Research Corporation. (2001, June). *Guide to quality: Even Start Family Literacy Program* (Vol. 1, rev.). Manuscript submitted for publication. Retrieved from http://www.state.nj.us/education/titles/title1/even/quality.pdf.

Townley, K. F., Heberle, J., & Kim, Y. K. (1988). *Proceedings from the 1987 Conference on Appalachia*. Lexington: Appalachian Center, University of Kentucky.

University of Kentucky Appalachian Center. (2010). *Parent and child education (PACE)*. Retrieved from http://appalachiancenter.org/node/209.

Wasik, B. H. (2004). Family literacy: History, concepts, services. In B. H. Wasik (Ed.), *Handbook of family literacy* (pp. 3–22). Mahwah, NJ: Lawrence Erlbaum Associates.

CHAPTER 7

What Are the Steps to Preparing a Family Literacy Event?

Preparing for a family literacy event begins with deciding where the first event will be held. In smaller cities or neighborhoods within larger cities, the decision depends upon what has gone on in the past. If your public library has an active adult literacy program with story times organized for parent education also, that library may be the best site. One consideration that has been learned over time with adult literacy programs is that many adults have had negative experiences with schools and would prefer to come to the library for a program. However, when this program involves their children, this should generate fewer concerns. When a larger crowd is anticipated, a local school may offer the needed space. In either case, it is a time for working together to get the maximum response from your intended audience. It always requires a team effort.

DEVELOP A TEAM

Now that you have seen the variety of benefits of hosting family literacy events and seen examples of what an event could look like at your public library or school library, the next step is to actually plan your own family literacy event. In this chapter, our aim is to provide the reader with a ready-to-use outline of the many steps to consider when planning a family literacy event. Specifically, you will be provided with appropriate checklists and step-by-step instructions to guide your planning efforts. In addition, both local public and school library literary and other community resources are considered for inclusion in this process. In doing so, the overall impact of a family literary event may be maximized with the greatest possible benefit to families and the greater local community.

Based on Sheneman's 2010 survey of librarians across America, it appears family literacy events are planned by a wide assortment of people including persons other than librarians: friends of the library groups, literacy coaches, reading specialists, reading vertical teams (across grade levels), site-based school leadership teams, faculty meeting attendees, and Parent Teacher Organizations (PTOs)/Parent Teacher Associations (PTAs). Some librarians have even opted to connect with their local community partners. One event was reported as being hosted at the public library but using the school librarian and teacher to read aloud their favorite books. The public library workers then pulled books with great reviews from the collection and encouraged participants to read for 45 to 60 minutes. Careful selection of the family literacy team that will plan your family literacy events is crucial. Whether you use volunteers or community members on your family literacy team, you need to consider them as participants in the event when you need additional help.

OTHER PROFESSIONALS AND VOLUNTEERS

It takes many people to pull off a successful family literacy event. When your team is planning the event, they will have a better idea of how many people are needed to host it even though you start as a one-person show. No matter what your situation entails, consider the possibility of asking for volunteers to support your family literacy event.

You will have many opportunities for professional personnel to be involved. Poll the public library staff or the school librarian to gather ideas of what skills teachers would like parents to practice at home to help improve children's reading skills. If a committee plans the events, they may decide to recruit staff members to develop activities associated with the selected titles or themes. If all the library staff and teachers attend the family literacy events, they are showing the families that they care about the children involved, and they serve as role models of adults who enjoy literature. It is also helpful to have other library staff and teachers be in charge of the sign-in tables and write on the name tags since they are familiar with the families and will be welcoming faces. Someone familiar with your library or school could be a helpful "runner" to get needed items quickly or escort people to the correct locations. At times you may hire a professional storyteller or performer. Remember there are many hidden talents among your own staff members or teachers at the school. Get to know them and find out their strengths.

Remember the wealth of assistance you can receive from volunteers, professional or nonprofessional. On one extreme, volunteers may help fund your event. Some restaurants or stores will provide free snacks and drinks. At times, their employees will need to be involved. Think about all the needs of your potential audience. Will you need a translator or a sign language interpreter? If so, a task-specific volunteer may be needed.

On a more practical, hands-on level, volunteers can help set up beforehand and clean up afterward. Depending on the size of your event, you may need help with crowd control or guiding families to meeting areas. Volunteers can help serve food. Be sure they have necessary supplies for good hygiene, like latex gloves. If you have activity stations or centers, well-trained volunteers can oversee these.

COMMUNITY INVOLVEMENT

Partnering with community groups can benefit both you and the community group. Many grant applications will ask you to list community partnerships. These partnerships come in a variety of formats. Some groups give financially, offer personnel manpower, provide giveaways and prizes, offer specialized services related to their field (income tax advice or diabetes screening), and a multitude of other services. Perhaps you live in an area where clubs reenact historical events. That could be an exciting thing for your families to experience. Building relationships within the community can have lasting impact on your school and its families.

Public librarians have reported partnering with their school librarians, especially when the public library is needed for a neutral or nonthreatening place to meet. A natural avenue for many schools is to recruit volunteers from the ranks of their PTA/PTO. Parents may volunteer themselves or have contacts through their employment or social contacts. Advertise the specific type of need you have and see if parents can help you make the community connections.

If you are fortunate enough to live in a city with a theme park or sports organization, ask about the community support they offer. Some provide reading incentives, such as a reading log students fill out and trade in for a ticket to a sporting event or park pass. Other teams may allow their athletes to visit your public library or the local school and give motivational talks or read to children. Check with your local Boys and Girls Club or YMCA. Some of these groups may offer free or discounted services for your group to use their facility for special events.

CHOOSING A TIME AND TOPIC

Once the family literacy team is selected, choosing a time and topic for your event is very important. The timing for your family literacy event can be a difficult decision. It will be handled differently if it is to be a single event or a weekly event held over several weeks. Your committee will need to be familiar with ongoing community events and special events in your area. Do not try to compete with events that may be important in your area, such as religious services or sporting events.

If you begin a series of family literacy events rather than a single event, you should have them on a regular schedule parents can plan for in advance just as they know the regular schedule for story time programs. For example, if you select the first Monday of the month, your families will know to set aside that day as they plan their family activities. Or, you could schedule your events to try to reach different populations, alternating between evenings and mornings. If the events are to be scheduled at the school, they might be held in conjunction with other school events such as open house, parent conferences, book fairs, or family picnics.

Another consideration is when to host the event. Have your committee discuss the working status of your families. Do you serve single-income families or large groups of unemployed parents? If so, then you may have great attendance for events held during the school day. Remember, too, these parents may have infants and toddlers who will need child care during your program(s) so they do not become a distraction or interruption.

For some, holding an event during the school year on a school day can be very successful. One school reported hosting events during the school day. The interest to the students was missing class time to be with their parents at the event. In the eyes of these students, they were missing out on class time. Little did they consider that they were still in an educational environment. They were now just in a class with their parents as fellow classmates.

If your families are busy during the school day, there are several options for you to consider according to Sheneman's survey (2010). Some librarians have family literacy events in the summer when children and parents potentially have relatively more time. Many librarians in the poll suggested Tuesdays and Thursdays evening with the idea that families were too tired on Mondays and ready to start their weekends on Fridays. A popular time was 6:00–8:00 P.M. Starting at 6 P.M. would allow parents time to leave work, pick up their families, and arrive at the event. Many suggested providing finger foods or snacks so hunger was not an issue. A few librarians suggested Saturday afternoons as a good meeting time. The family literacy team needs to be intimately familiar with your target audience.

Choosing a topic is a major decision. If the topic is not interesting and engaging, then it will not draw an audience and all of the planning will go to waste. The survey (Sheneman, 2010) showed some librarians selected a topic of interest to the children. These librarians knew by building children or student interest, the excitement could possibly spill over to the family.

Sometimes themes were chosen that were topics of interest for the age group or community. For example, one librarian chose pets and the animal shelter. By combining these topics, the librarian was able to garner the children's interest in pets and tie it in to the community issue of animal shelters. At other times, themes were chosen that reflected the time of the year or upcoming events in the community.

Other librarians took a more academic approach and based their event on their school board's or school's literacy initiatives, which were tied to needs identified by academic data (Sheneman, 2010). They looked at test scores and planned an evening with a theme that incorporated reading and a particular skill, like comprehension, that was weak according to the aggregated data. One mentioned hosting planning meetings with the people they wanted to target for the event, both adults and children. These individuals helped to choose a specific focus and date, and an overall plan.

PLANNING SHEET

As with most events, detailed planning is of upmost importance. Carefully developing a family literacy team can lead to the development of a planning sheet for a successful event that can be replicated many times at your library or school. Talking with others who have already hosted family literacy events will help ensure you

Public Library Planning Sheet

Age Level _____

Date _____

Theme/Title _____

"Free" Person to Oversee _____

Duties	Assigned to:
GETTING READY	
invitations, posters, and flyers ~ approved by administration before printing	
phone number list of regular attendees sent to volunteer phone contact ~ one week in advance	
sign-in sheet and handouts printed	
name tags/labels	
purchase drinks, paper goods, and supplies	
call food provider to preorder	
collect raffle items	
DAY OF EVENT	
leave custodian a Post-It note on his door to set up coffee and room arrangement	
man sign-in table	
cut up sign-in sheets for raffle	

Figure 7.1: Sample Public Library Planning Sheet

Team Time Planning Sheet

Grade Level _____

Date _____

Theme/Title _____

"Free" Person to Oversee _____

Duties	Assigned to:
invitations ~ approved by principal before printing	
phone list to parent center ~ one week in advance	
sign-in sheet and parent rotation handout	
name tags/labels	
man sign-in table	
leave custodian a Post-It note on his door to set up coffee and pizza serving tables	
order sweetbread ~ give receipt to secretary	
set up sweetbread table in the morning	
contact cafeteria ~ sack lunches or Styrofoam trays needed	
purchase drinks and paper goods ~ check with secretary	
call pizza place to warn of upcoming orders	
copy attendance rosters and order pizzas	
pass out pizza	
communicate with coach the type of family activity desired	
signal/announce "time to rotate"	
collect raffle items	
cut up sign-in sheets for raffle	
purchase students giveaways for all students	
prepare raffle and giveaway bags	

Activities Planned:	Presented By:	Location:	Rotation Times:
Registration		Cafeteria	8:30 – 8:45
Welcome	principal	Cafeteria	8:45 – 9:00
1.			9:00 – 9:45
2.			9:45 – 10:30
3.			10:30 – 11:15
Family Game Time	coach	Gym	11:15 – 11:45
Lunch		Patio	11:45 – 12:15

Assignments to cover classrooms with students not in attendance:

_____

Figure 7.2: Sample School Library Planning Sheet

From *Crash Course in Family Literacy Programs* by Rosemary Chance and Laura Sheneman. Santa Barbara, CA: Libraries Unlimited. Copyright © 2012.

have planned for everything you need. Careful planning can also help prevent many potential disasters or uncomfortable moments during the actual event itself. Once you have brainstormed all the areas you will need to plan for, create a planning guide that becomes an event guide. Creating a planning guide should be done as a collaborative effort, with the team members assisting in the event. This is particularly necessary when staff in a small public library or a branch of a larger library system is limited and when working with a nearby elementary school means only one school librarian and fewer teachers.

This planning guide can be a simple Microsoft Word document or Excel spreadsheet that lists all pieces of the program, the timeline, what is needed for that portion of the plan, and who will be responsible for each segment. For example, who will create and send out invitations? Who will recruit volunteers? Who will oversee child care for infants and toddlers who are not involved in the event? Notice the level of detail on the sample planning sheet.

Do not leave anything to chance. It is better to overplan than have empty time with your families who committed time and effort to plan your event. The following sample planning sheets show you the amount of thought and details one school completed to ensure everything was accounted for, including the timing.

Delegating responsibilities will help share the work load and will result in a less stressful experience for all involved. Having a family literacy team will allow more eyes to proof publicity and review the calendar to be sure there are fewer conflicts with other events. Several respondents (Sheneman, 2010) mentioned planning meetings where they delegated the responsibilities to the family literacy team and another meeting to check in with each other to be sure everything is taken care of prior to the event. Based on the size of your family literacy team, you might discover the need for volunteers or additional team members. This is the time to seek help from your Friends of the Library group or another local volunteer group. After hosting one or two events, come back as a team and review the planning guide. Make modifications as your team sees fit.

CHOICE OF MATERIALS FOR FAMILY LITERACY EVENT

Many times family literacy events are based around a single book title rather than a theme. Choose your title wisely. The choice may be made for you if you are following a purchased program or curriculum or if you receive guidance from a literacy committee or local literacy council. If your events are planned around a book club idea for older children and with parents who are able to read the chosen book, then you will have all participants read the same book, so title selection will not be a concern. For example, "One Book" community reading programs often culminate in a large group literacy event.

Some librarians (Sheneman, 2010) mentioned hosting events based on books with movie tie-ins. You have several options with this. If your families are reading the title as a book club, then you could culminate in an event where the families enjoy a movie and popcorn night. If you show the movie at school, you should consider issues related to copyright. Services are available for you to purchase that will give you a performance site license to show movies for noneducational purposes, such as Movie Licensing USA.

When considering a title, there are several things to bear in mind. If you planned a themed event, use your Online Public Access Catalog (OPAC) to help you find theme-related titles. For example, if your theme or genre was fairy tales, then you should select books that feature various fairy tales. If you are hosting the event in conjunction with a book fair, you will want to showcase titles for sale in your fair. If your target audience is all male, consider searching Jon Scieszka's website *Guys Read* (http://www.guysread.com/) to find an appealing title. Struggling readers may be attracted to high interest books. Seasonal events could feature seasonal book titles. For example, a December family literacy event could showcase holiday stories from around the world. If you have the freedom to choose, you will want to choose a title connected to your planned audience. Picture books can be attractive to most ages, but choose with thought of the oldest student you expect, as well.

The following chapter will offer a few sample activities. The Internet and other printed resources are filled with ideas you can use for your family literacy event. Remember also the expertise you have at your local schools. With a little searching, you will find activities that fit your literacy goals. There is no need to reinvent the wheel.

Figure 7.3: Sample Movie Night Advertisement Held in a School Auditorium

PUBLICITY

Planning a fantastic event will be no good if you do little to advertise your event. Your publicity should have an eye-catching name to get your families attention. Some teams choose a themed name such as "Blooming in Kinder" that will coordinate with announcement clip art, name tags, workshop titles, and snacks. Parents will need to know the day, time, location, and a contact person in case they have any questions. Include any special interest information like a gathering time with coffee and pastries shortly before the event begins. Mention other attention-getting information such as door prizes, babysitting services for infants and toddlers, or food. These announcements will show parents you have planned well and have taken care of many things that will make their attendance easier and more fun.

You can advertise onsite through typical means like bulletin boards, marquees, banners, door posters, handouts on the public library circulation desk, and even word

Figure 7.4: Inside View of Sample Parent Invitation

of mouth. Another tool is printed messages designed for children to take home from school or day care. These printed announcements could take on the format of a simple flyer or school newsletter. You should consider your need to create these flyers with a cut-off response requesting RSVP information and whether you need bilingual fliers to reach all of your parents. If you have a parent liaison or someone assigned to connect with your families, ask them to call the targeted parents and give a verbal invitation.

In our world filled with so many modern technologies, you have a multitude of means to invite people to attend your family literacy event. Many librarians in public libraries and schools have taken advantage of social networking tools such as Facebook, Twitter, and blogs to send out mass communications to their families and patrons. Your library may have access to automated phone messaging or texting system. Others choose Web page notices and group e-mail send-outs.

When your event is over, consider sending a short article with photos to your local newspaper. If time allows in your preplanning, assign someone to invite local newspapers or television stations to attend your event and showcase to the community the incredible work you are doing. This kind of advertising will build community support for your programs and possibly get the attention of future funders you may wish to contact as your program blooms and flourishes in the future.

FUNDING

At some point, funding your family literacy event may be an issue. Whether funding plans come before or after you develop your family literacy team and planned the event, at some point you will have to determine your funding needs and funding source. Remember, if you are writing a grant for your family literacy event(s), you will need to provide this information for your budget breakdown. Several things need to be included in your funding plan.

1. What supplies will your family literacy team need for the event itself?
2. Will you have advertising expenses?
3. Will you provide snacks and drinks?
4. Will there be child care expenses?
5. Will you have raffles, door prizes, or giveaways?

You can find a variety of ways to fund family literacy events. Talk to your principal if you are considering hosting a family literacy event. Many have learned to be very creative with their annual budget or in using the budget provided by the local school district. Public librarians may be able to apply for Library Services and Technology Act (LSTA) funding from their state library or, working with the school librarian, they may be able to use Title I funds from the government, which allow for parental involvement, or include parental involvement monies on their own. By demonstrating how your event focuses on parents, you may be eligible to use these funds.

Speak to your library director. Money within your own library budget could be used to fund your event. Keep in mind that a new line item in the budget may have to be created, and this may take some time to get approved. Be sure to ask well in advance.

Fundraising is one funding source. The use of money from fundraisers is often not restricted to approved vendors since it is not part of actual budgeted monies. In schools, student activity funds or campus activity funds are monies raised or collected and spent to support the school's activities for all students. These funds often result from fundraising the students do themselves. However, some students might be interested in raising money for a family literacy program.

Typical school library fundraisers include profits from book fairs. Several book fairs offer cash profits, which some schools add to their student activity funds. Since many items your planning team will spend money on for family literacy events are not tied in to any vendors, fundraising is a wonderful avenue to follow. It can be challenging to blend funding for the public library and schools, but it does show a buy-in from both agencies for the very important project of developing family literacy.

Donations can also be a valuable resource. Sometimes local businesses will donate cash or specific items related to their place of business. Larger chain stores will often have a website with a community relations section. Read about the businesses in your area. You may be able to request free pizza, doughnuts, or beverages. Food is always a good way to attract an audience, and anything free is great for your budget! Consider, also, asking your Friends of the Library group, or ask your school librarian to request funding from the school's PTA/PTO for assistance. You can request funds from any of these groups, but keep in mind the funds would typically have to be approved at a meeting, so request these funds well in advance. At other times, you may have a local business or organization sponsor your event in other ways. Maybe your local Boys and Girls Club will work with you as a hosting site if their space would work better than the public library or school. Think creatively and you may come up with several ways for others to partner with you.

ASSESSMENT

Assessing your event is vitally important. If you desire to assess the educational impact of your family literacy program, you must first decide what exactly you want to assess.

For preschool children, your questions will involve changes in parents reading to their children at home and changes in attention span of children and recognition of letters of the alphabet. The length of time children will sit quietly may also be something that will increase. Their wanting to spend time listening to a story or looking at a picture book by themselves also indicates steps toward literacy.

For older children, if you want to see if family literacy can increase children's attitudes about reading, you could consider using a questionnaire similar to the Elementary Reading Attitude Survey (ERAS) developed by McKenna and Kear (1990). If you simply want to know if the children are reading more, a reading log could be created to see if the children who participate in your family literacy events read more over time when compared to children who did not participate in your events. The more specific your goal is from the beginning, the more accurate your assessment feedback will be.

The results of your assessment can help you plan future events. You will want to repeat things that were successful and re-plan for content or sections that did not run as smoothly. At times you may need to collect results of some kind to provide accountability to funding partners or to boards who oversee you, such as school boards or library boards. Keeping accurate records will also provide excellent evidence for grants and funding applications. For example, if you desire to increase the amount time children are read to at home, create a simple survey to send home prior to the family literacy event. Then resend it several months later to see if any changes occurred.

Many ways are available to assess your family literacy events. Think back to the goals your family literacy team put in place. If your goal was to increase parent participation, a simple sign-in sheet will provide documentation for counting the number of actual attendees. Keep accurate records of attendance. These records can reveal many things, including when interest began to wane as would be indicated by lower attendance and retention changes.

When you want feedback about the event from the parents' perspective, you can create a survey parents fill out at the end of each session. You will probably receive more responses if you ask for the surveys to be filled out on the spot rather than be returned at a later date. Depending on the population you serve, you may need to have the survey translated into multiple languages. You need to decide if your survey will be online, with a free survey maker like Surveymonkey, or on paper. If you have time, you can verbally talk with families after the event to gather feedback. They can tell you on the spot what worked or did not work, what was appealing or not appealing, and

---

Child's Name _____   Nombre de Niño(a):   _____
Grade _____   Nivel: _____

1. How often do you read to your child at home?   1. ¿Con qué frecuencia le lee a su hijo(a) en la casa?
       __ never   __ nunca
       __1 or 2 times a week   __ 1 o 2 veces por la semana
       __3-4 times a week   __ 3-4 veces por la semana
       __ 5-6 times a week   __ 5-6 veces por la semana
       __every day   __ Todos los días

2. How often do you listen to your child read at   2. ¿Con qué frecuencia usted escucha a su hijo(a)
home?   leer en la casa?
       __ never   __ Nunca
       __1 or 2 times a week   __ 1 o 2 veces por la semana
       __3-4 times a week   __ 3-4 veces por la semana
       __ 5-6 times a week   __ 5-6 veces por la semana
       __every day   __ todos los días

Figure 7.5: Sample Form to Track Impact on Reading to a Child at Home

what they wish you could provide at future events. In addition, talking with students the day after the event will provide feedback about future attendance, interest in other programming ideas, and parent reactions.

It is also important to check in with your family literacy team. Have a short meeting after the event to find out what worked smoothly and what needs to be sharpened up for future events. Discuss problems that occurred and brainstorm possible

Event: _____   Date: _____   Time: _____

Parent's Name/ Nombre del Padre	Child's Name/ Nombre del Niño/Niña

Figure 7.6: Sample Sign-in Sheet

First-Grade Parent Meeting - Evaluation Responses
10-15-09

1. **What was your favorite part of this Parent Meeting?**

   - Seeing every teacher doing their best to educate every parent today.
   - Spending time at school with my child and learning ways to help teach my child.
   - Learning different ways to help my kids at home.
   - Everything was good.
   - Being with the school staff and learning.
   - Participating with the child. I like the child and parent being together.

2. **What was your least favorite part?**

   - Don't have one.
   - It was too short.
   - Sessions were too short.
   - Didn't have one.
   - I loved everything.
   - Going to gym.
   - There was no least favorite part due to everything was covered.

3. **Do you have any suggestions for future Parent Meetings?**

   - Not at this time.
   - I think these should be done more often throughout the year.
   - More meetings through the year and more time.
   - Maybe more "hands-on" experiences.
   - Would like to spend more time in each class.
   - Maybe try to make it longer.

4. **Topics I would like address in the future are:**

   - Learn more about recycling.
   - Study skills and computer literacy.
   - How to help the kids learn faster.
   - How to keep them more focused and how to keep them in school.

5. **One think I learned today was:**

   - Being responsible for my children.
   - Science is all around us.
   - How to spend more time to read with your child, and to be more responsible with their work.
   - How the teachers are devoted in the development of our children.
   - That coming to the parent meeting is very important to all of us.
   - To have more ideas to do activities with my child.
   - How to help my child at home understand "teachable moments."

Figure 7.7: Sample Parent Feedback

solutions. For example, perhaps you needed a bilingual interpreter or a babysitter for rowdy toddlers while you worked with parents and older elementary students. Examine the parent survey responses to evaluate the feedback you received. Use these responses to guide a discussion with the family literacy team. A quick glance at the sample in Figure 7.7 reveals several praises to pump your team up and also offers some suggestions as you plan future events. These kinds of surveys are also helpful because they provide some evidence and verbal feedback to use when you are seeking funding or providing documentation of your successes to your funding agency.

The Figure 7.7 results were obtained from a written survey asking parents for feedback from an event held in a school. Notice the parents share both the good and bad from the event. This kind of feedback is vital for improvement of future literacy events. Based on the responses shared, program planners have a multitude of things to consider. In this instance, the organization offered one family event per grade level each year. For example, a kindergarten event in September, a first grade event in October, a second grade event in November, and so on. The participants in this example expressed an interest in more offerings per grade level. A multitude of responses covered lengthening the amount time spent in sessions. It seemed the 45 minute sessions did not offer the length of time parents needed.

CONCLUSION

In conclusion, there are many steps that must be in place to host a successful family literacy event. Once you get your literacy team and planning sheet in place, choose the perfect meeting time, and select the best material, you are ready to recruit some fantastic personnel, volunteers, and community agencies. Next, you need to publicize in every way and means possible. When needed, look for outside funding. Remember to decide what you want to assess during the planning stages. If you have done careful assessment, you will have documentation to provide to potential funders and ideas to improve your program in the future. When all the steps are in place, you are well on your way to a bright future of meeting the needs of your patrons, both the children and their families.

References

McKenna, M. C., & Kear, D. J. (1990). Measuring attitude towards reading: A new tool for teachers. *The Reading Teacher, 43*, 626–639.

Sheneman, L. C. (2010). *Family literacy survey*. Retrieved from http://www.survey monkey.com/sr.aspx?sm=cftN8zqu4WaOWxS9d97RUbQQhpd1iNcJo4Ju2_2b8j xm0_3d.

CHAPTER 8

What Is the Role of Parent-Child Literacy Interaction and Parent Education?

Think back to an earlier definition of family literacy as stated by Wasik (2004); the basic principle of family literacy programs is "the intergenerational transmission of literacy from one family member to another" (p. 619). When considering the population you work with, you may wonder how the families of your patrons could successfully be able to pass on literacy skills to their children when the adults seem to have weak literacy skills of their own. You may believe something similar to Darling (2004): "A child from a welfare family would have to participate slightly more than 8 hours a day, 5 days a week, in some sort of intervention program that provided language-rich instruction with adults, to have experiences similar to their more advantaged peers" (p. 608). You may believe some school-age children are in educational environments that are not language rich or high quality. Providing family literacy programming to these children may increase their success (Darling, 2004, p. 608) if it is ongoing and of high quality.

This transference of knowledge can be accomplished by using family adults to demonstrate, model, and guide children in literacy-related activities. A family literacy team can help train parents in simple tasks to do at home when working with their children. These tasks can be learned and practiced in your library setting. Then parents will be enabled to repeat the tasks at home with their child. It is of vital importance to show parents that literacy development occurs in the everyday activities of home life. Changing routines and study habits can aid this learning process.

One way to respect differences between parents and yourself is to provide announcements, handouts, and other related items in the parents' home language. The family literacy team should be aware not all parents grew up in homes where literacy was supported and encouraged. They may be unaware of simple things they can do with their child to build early literacy skills. For example, do your parents know having storybooks present in the home is important (Wasik, 2004, p. 624)? Your family literacy team can brainstorm ways to increase the number of books in your families' homes through grant writing, encouraging public library use, collecting community donations, and making homemade books.

A variety of ways encourage families to place greater importance on literacy skills in their daily lives. The public library or school setting can serve as a conduit for this type of information. Make it a goal to train parents and families to incorporate new literacy-related skills in their homes. Hosting literacy events at your library can be an ideal situation to see new behaviors modeled, practice these new skills under the guidance of experts, and make plans to apply these skill sets in their own homes. These literacy events can be hosted any time of day when your patrons and their families are available: morning for toddlers and preschoolers, during school time during the school year if you have a captive audience of students and parents, evenings after the parents' work day, Saturdays, or even days in the summer when families may be looking for children's activities. As you plan, bear in mind there are two potential focal points for literacy events: parent-child literacy interactions or parenting education and support.

PARENT-CHILD LITERACY INTERACTIONS

Remember the federal government's four components of a family literacy program: early childhood education, adult education, parenting education and support, and parent-child literacy interactions. This section will focus on the idea of family literacy events as the means to provide parent-child literacy interactions. Hosting a family literacy event can be as simple as a family story time event that creates opportunities for parent-child literacy interactions. However, instead of simply having a story time and a snack, try offering a story time that includes parent training related to their interactions with the child. This is the focus of the Association for Library Service to Children (ALSC), a division of the American Library Association (ALA). Their Every Children Ready to Read program is in its second edition and is available on the ALA website.

Brainstorm skills you consider vital to literacy. Work with a local teacher to select a story to promote a skill you consider vital to develop literacy. If you feel at a loss, do a search online to discover lists of literacy skills. You will find things for younger students like awareness of the sounds of language, awareness of print, and the relationship between letters and sounds. For older students you will see vocabulary, spelling, and comprehension.

The samples found on the following pages can be modified to fit your goals and needs. Notice thought was given to identify several key points: the literacy goal for students/children, the goal for parents to understand, a time for modeling and independent practice, and a plan for what you want the parents to do once they go home. Formulate plans to train the family adults to demonstrate, model, and guide their children in literacy-related activities in their own homes. Model the idea of purposeful interactions so that they can emulate you in their own homes. Consider items such as magnetic take-home checklists in families' native languages to serve as a visual reminder to practice intentional interactions with their children. A simple take-home memento can go a long way in prompting their memory at home to practice what they learned.

SAMPLE PARENT-CHILD LITERACY INTERACTION PLANS

The following are sample book titles and related activities that you can consider using for your parent-child literacy interactions. These activities can be implemented with minimal preparation on your part. Many of the titles will remind you of other titles you might be familiar with. Be creative and spin off your own ideas based on the titles you know. Each sample event below follows a simple template that you can reuse for your own planning. The template includes:

1. Book information
2. Goal for students/children
3. Goal for parents: What do you want them to *understand?*
4. Approximate time needed
5. Supplies needed
6. Family literacy event description
7. Conclusion: What do you urge the parents to *do* with what they learned from you?

Jackson, Alison, 2002. *I Know an Old Lady Who Swallowed a Pie*. Puffin. Illustrated by Judy Schachner. (Paperback) ISBN-10: 0140565957 ISBN-13: 978-0140565959

Grade level(s): Kindergarten, first, second
Submitted by: Cathy Amrhein

Goal for students/children: Recognize rhythm and pattern in story, predict ending, create alternative story endings.

Goal for parents: What do you want them to *understand?* Story time can be fun; nonreaders can participate in story time with rhyming word prediction and repeated patterns. Also, parents can use stories for creative problem solving by creating alternate endings.

Approximate time needed: 1 hour

Supplies needed: Name tags and pens, multimedia projector and screen, a copy of book *There Was an Old Lady Who Swallowed a Pie*, butcher paper, wide-tipped marker. Buckets for each table containing: construction paper, markers/crayons, highlight tape, at least two different versions of Jackson's *There Was an Old Lady* books (e.g., *There Was an Old Lady Who Swallowed a Bell* and *There Was an Cold Lady Who Swallowed Some Snow*).

Family Literacy Event Description

10 minutes

Arrival and opening: As families arrive, have audio CD of the music/story *There Was an Old Lady Who Swallowed a Fly* playing on speakers. This will familiarize all parents and children with the stories sing-song rhythm. Have parents make name tags for each family member.

5 minutes

Introduction: Introduce yourself and explain goals for this literacy night. Talk about author, Alison Jackson, and explain this series of books are a play off the well-known "There was an old lady who swallowed a fly . . ." nursery rhyme. Show examples of her stories (*There Was an Old Lady Who Swallowed a Bell, There Was an Old Lady Who Swallowed Some Sand.*)

5 minutes

Model lesson—Rhyming: Use projector screen and read the first few pages of *There Was an Old Lady Who Swallowed a Pie*. While reading, ask children to predict what word fits the end of the sentence using rhyming word cues. Highlight the rhyming words with highlight tape. Explain each page has a pair of rhyming words. Talk about how the letters at the ends of the words are the same and that's what makes them rhyme. Allow some children to come to the projector to highlight rhyming words. **Do not read the ending of the story.**

5 minutes

Prediction: Use projector screen, reread story one page at a time. Model how to lead their children to guess what's going to happen next to the old lady in the story. "What will she swallow next? Does she have any more room? What other things do you have at Thanksgiving? Is she going to eat more?" When you get to the end of the story, brainstorm ideas of how the story may end. Write their ideas on a piece of paper at the front of the room, encourage anything and everything—the sillier the better (this activity models writing and allows children to see value of their spoken word). Read the end of the story and see if any guesses were right.

5 minutes

Alternate ending: Brainstorm alternate endings to this story, make sure the ideas match the descriptions in the story (i.e., must be related to Thanksgiving).

20 minutes

Independent practice: On the projector, list the activities for the parents to do using another one of Alison Jackson's stories. Remind them to: (1) work on rhyming while using the highlighter tape, (2) predict throughout the story, and (3) brainstorm with their children for alternate endings. Have them record their predictions and endings on a piece of construction paper. If time allows, when a family completes their three tasks, they may find another story of rhyming verses and attempt the three skills they have learned. Once everyone is done, have the families share their funniest predictions.

After all groups are done, collect the papers to make into a small book to share in the library. Have students make a cover page for the book and you write an explanation of literacy night inside the cover. Show the children the book the following week to give them positive feedback and rewarding compliments on their attendance and hard work.

10 minutes

Conclusion: What do you urge the parents to *do* with what they learned from you?

This literacy night should help parents realize reading is fun and interactive. They can take any easy reader story and find rhyming words, predict next event, or create alternate stories. When you read to your children every day, use at least one of these skills to make the story more interesting and help your children be more involved.

Cain, Janan. 2000. *The Way I Feel*. Parenting Press. (Hardcover) ISBN-10: 9781884734717 ISBN-13: 978-1884734717

Available in Spanish *Asi Me Siento Yo,* ISBN-10: 1884734839 ISBN-13: 978-1884734830

Grade level(s): Kindergarten, first, second

Submitted by: Cathy Amrhein

Goal for students/children: Think about how emotions make them feel.

Goal for parents: What do you want them to *understand*? Everyone has emotions and we need to talk about our emotions. This lesson will help children find the words to express their feelings with words. Parents will understand that books can serve as bridges to conversation starters.

Approximate time needed: 1 hour

Supplies needed: Name tags, pens, butcher paper, wide-tipped marker, copy of the story for each family or a list of emotions discussed in the story. A bucket for each table containing: a mirror, a stapler, white copy paper, markers, crayons, pens, pencils, erasers, one piece of construction paper per family.

Family Literacy Event Description

10 minutes

Arrival and opening: As families arrive, have audio CD of kid's music playing on speakers. Allow children to dance around to the music and encourage them to change their dance with the "feel" of the music. Have parents make name tags for each family member.

5 minutes

Introduction: Ask "Did you enjoy dancing to the music? How did it make you feel?" Introduce yourself and explain goals for this literacy night. Brainstorm with families to find a definition of "emotion"; record ideas on a piece of butcher paper. Ask a few leading questions such as: "Are emotions ok? Is it okay to be mad? Is it ok to be sad?" Introduce the story *The Way I Feel* by Janan Cain.

5 minutes

Read *The Way I Feel* aloud to group. Make sure everyone can see illustrations. You may want to project the story on the overhead screen for easy viewing.

5 minutes

Model lesson: Go back to the beginning of the story and ask everyone to show you the face they would make when they felt silly. Pass the mirrors around the table to watch their own faces. As a group, brainstorm what you would do when you feel silly, or what makes you feel silly. Show the "scared" page and ask everyone to show each other their scared faces. Encourage families to talk with each other about faces and emotions.

Again, brainstorm what you would do when you feel scared, or what makes you feels scared.

10 minutes

Independent practice: On a large piece of paper or projector, write the three jobs for parents to do with story: (1) Make faces for each emotion; (2) Ask your child, "How would you describe that feeling?"; (3) Ask you child, "What things makes you feel that way?"

Ask the families to go through the rest of the book's emotions and practice making the faces, talk about what they do when they feel that way, and what type of things make them feel that emotion.

15 minutes

Activity: Explain to the group that they are going to make a book about emotions. Write your last name across a piece of construction paper. Next, take a white copy page and write one emotion at the top of the page (for example, "joy") and draw what your face looks like when you feel joy. Write or draw a few events that make you feel that way. Explain that each family is now going to make their own book. Give each table a bucket of supplies. Ask each family to take one piece of construction paper and write their family name in large letters on one side. Ask each family member to take one piece of white copy paper and record their favorite emotion from the book or one that is not in the book. When done, they should use their construction paper as the title page and make a book of their family's emotion pages. Ask the families to read the story together.

If time allows, ask for volunteers to share their family books. They can either take their books home or you can make copies of each page to make a library copy combining all emotions in one book.

10 minutes

Conclusion: What do you urge the parents to *do* with what they learned from you? Families have now opened the door to discuss emotions and know that emotions are okay to feel. Parents know that books can be used to start discussions about important issues as well as serve as bridges to important conversations with their children. Talking about emotions will also help build vocabulary words to describe feelings and develop open communication in the home.

Cronin, Doreen. 2000. *Click, Clack, Moo: Cows that Type.* Illustrated by Betsy Lewin. Little Simon. (Paperback) ISBN-10: 1442433701 ISBN-13: 978-1442433700

Available in Spanish *Clic, Clac, Muu: Vacas Escritoras;* ISBN-10: 1417745142 ISBN-13: 978-1417745142

Grade level(s): Second, third

Submitted by: Cathy Amrhein

Goal for students/children: Retell a story; present dramatic interpretations of experiences, stories, poems, or plays.

Goal for parents: What do you want them to *understand?* Children can act out stories for fun or to offer new experiences for families.

Approximate time needed: 1 hour

Supplies needed: *Click, Clack, Moo: Cows that Type,* projector, camera, art supply bucket for each table containing glue sticks; black, red, yellow and white construction paper; paper plates; popsicle sticks or handle for plate mask; sample masks for display.

Family Literacy Event Description

5 minutes

Arrival and opening: Have a variety of puppets and masks on the tables for families to explore and play with. When you are ready to begin, ask children to bring puppets and masks back to one area in library.

5 minutes

Introduction: Introduce yourself and explain goals for this literacy night. Read *Click, Clack, Moo: Cows that Type* aloud to large group. Use projector if possible so entire room can see illustrations.

20 minutes

Art project: Explain that they will make masks to use when they recreate the story. Show bucket of supplies and a few models of masks you made already. Pass out table buckets. Make sure each table makes a farmer, a cow, a hen, and a duck mask. Allow time to finish masks. Take photos during the project creation. Have everyone clean up their areas and put unused supplies back in the buckets. Have children bring buckets back to front of the room.

20 minutes

Dramatic response: Explain you will now reread the story and you would like to see everyone act out the part that corresponds to the mask they created. Mention at the end of the story you may ask for volunteers to retell the story with their own words.

Reread the story and have the participants stand up and act out the parts of the story. Ask if any groups would be comfortable reenacting the story using their own words. You may have to encourage children to work together to reenact the story. Call on children who regularly participate during your library time. Take photos during presentations.

After all groups are done, take pictures of the masked families to make into a small book to share in the library. Have children make a cover page for the book and you write an explanation of literacy night inside the cover. Show the children the book the following week to give them positive feedback and rewarding compliments on their attendance and hard work.

10 minutes

Conclusion: What do you urge the parents to *do* with what they learned from you?

This literacy night should help parents realize reading is fun and interactive. Children can act out stories for fun or to offer new experiences for families. Dramatic reenactments can be fun for the whole family. Role play allows everyone a chance to say or do things they may not be able to accomplish without props.

Cloudy with a Chance of Meatballs. 2009. Directed by Phil Lord and Chris Miller. Run time: 90 minutes. Rated: PG. Available with English, French, or Spanish subtitles. ASIN: B001UV4XY2

Movie Night

Grade level(s): First through fifth

Submitted by: Cathy Amrhein

Goal for children: Compare and contrast story versus movie events. Stories allow our imaginations to run free. Families enjoy free movie and popcorn event.

Goal for parents: What do you want them to *understand?* Movies can be educationally beneficial. Families have fun reading a story together then watching the movie. Families can compare the events and characters of the book with those in the movie. Also, families can critically think about plots in books versus movies and realize the development needed for each media.

Approximate time needed: 2.4 hours

Supplies needed: *Cloudy with a Chance of Meatballs* story and movie (make sure you purchase the license to show movie, which can be for a one time showing or an annual license such as Movie Licensing USA), butcher paper, wide-tipped markers, On Time coupon for M&M's, popcorn, popcorn bags, snack-sized M&M's, puzzles, blank paper and pencils on tables.

Family Literacy Event Description

5 minutes

Arrival and opening: Pass out On Time coupon for M&M's, puzzles on tables for parents to entertain children while waiting for event to begin. Clean puzzles up and bring them to one location to avoid distraction during event.

5 minutes

Introduction: Introduce self and goal of literacy night. Explain that you will read the story book first and discuss the characters and timeline of events. Next, they'll watch the movie and then discuss characters and timeline of events.

10 minutes

Read *Cloudy with a Chance of Meatballs*. On top of paper write "BOOK" and on one side of a piece of butcher paper write "Characters." Go back through the story and list all of the characters. On the other side write "Timeline" and quickly write a brief list of events in order of occurrence. Remind families that after the movie, you will write a list of characters and timeline as well. Encourage them to take notes during the movie.

90 minutes

Watch movie. Pass out popcorn as previews show to allow time to settle down, allow students to turn in their On Time coupons for M&M's at the same time or have a runner that will help pass out popcorn to all families as well as candy to on-time participants.

5 minutes

Have children throw trash away and stand up to stretch.

10 minutes

On one side of another piece of butcher paper write "MOVIE" at the top, then "Characters," and on the other side "Timeline." Help brainstorm list of all characters remembered as well as a quick list of events that happened during movie.

10 minutes

Model lesson: Starting with the movie characters, ask for families to name any characters both in the movie and in the book. As they begin to note very little similarity, ask why there are more characters in the movie. (Things need to be added to make movie longer, more interesting, etc.). After reviewing movie list of characters, check back on the book side and see if any of the book characters were in the movie. Again, ask if anyone cares to share their opinion of why the characters are different.

10 minutes

Independent practice: Ask the families to work together to list the similarities and differences in the movie and the book as far as events occur. After five minutes of brainstorming, bring group back together and lead in discussion of similarities and differences.

5 minutes

Application: Guide discussion to compare book and movie contents. Help families realize the plot is much more developed in a long movie whereas a short story has a simpler plot.

10 minutes

Conclusion: What do you urge the parents to *do* with what they learned from you? Encourage parents to read books before they watch the movies. Help their children compare the plots and characters to achieve higher level thinking skills.

Conclusion

A multitude of book titles are available for you to use for your family literacy events. These samples were meant to spark your own creativity. While they template may seem basic, it provides the simple framework to consider when planning the details of your event. When you are ready to branch out with your activities, look to some of the award-winning book lists available online. Consider Caldecott Medal winners when you are looking for quality picture books. Remember, also, awards that recognize the cultures of your patrons, such as the Belpré Medal (Latino/Latina authors and illustrators) or the Coretta Scott King Book Award (African American authors and illustrators).

PARENTING EDUCATION AND SUPPORT

Your public library may be too small to host larger groups of parents and their children. If you have contact with school or community resources and personnel to add another component to your family literacy events, consider adding parenting education and support. Perhaps you have access to a school or community counselor, a school or local reading specialist, a nurse, or other people who could address the education needs of your parents. Parenting education and support is another one of the federal government's four components of a family literacy program: early childhood education, adult education, parenting education and support, and parent-child literacy interactions.

The following scenario explains how Jefferson Elementary School in Harlingen, Texas, found ways to meet the needs of its families. Jefferson Elementary is in a low-income, Spanish language–dominant neighborhood in south Texas. The principal, Manuel Olivo, believed it was the school's responsibility to educate their parents in ways to get involved in their children's lives. A team was developed to create a plan to draw the parents into the school to participate in training sessions called Team Time. These parents had not been in the habit of frequently visiting the school, except to drop off and pick up their children.

The team developed a plan called Team Time to focus on the parents of one grade level a month. They developed a schedule that would allow the parents to rotate through training sessions. They determined that in order to encourage participation, they needed to find something to increase the parents' interest in this kind of event. It was decided that the sessions would be designed for both parents and children. In effect, the school used the students to encourage their parents to attend Team Time. If the parent attended the session, the students were allowed to join the parents in the session rotation during school hours.

The sessions were developed for the parents to visit: (1) the counselor/nurse who addressed information related to their specialization and training, (2) the reading specialist who discussed age-related reading information, and (3) classroom teachers who shared information and lead activities about skills important for their child's grade level.

The schedule in Table 8.1 shows how their rotation worked. The basis of this form was reused for each grade level's family literacy event. On the rows labeled 1, 2, and 3, the activity name, person presenting, and location were filled in for each grade level's event.

Table 8.1: Parent Rotation Planning Chart

Activities planned	Presented by	Location	Rotation times
Registration		Cafeteria	8:30–8:45 A.M.
Welcome	Mr. Olivo	Cafeteria	8:45–9:00 A.M.
1.			9:00–9:45 A.M.
2.			9:45–10:30 A.M.
3.			10:30–11:15 A.M.
Family Game Time	Coach	Gym	11:15–11:45 A.M.
Lunch		Patio	11:45–12:15 P.M.

You will notice they gathered in the cafeteria first. The parents signed in, got a name tag and rotation schedule, and enjoyed coffee and *pan dulce* (Mexican pastry bread). Meanwhile, they watched a video produced by the librarian showcasing all the students from that particular grade. The goal was to showcase their children hard at work and having fun at school. After a welcome from the principal, the parents were separated into three rotation groups as indicated by their name tags.

The rotation groups were determined as the parents signed in. They were assigned to one of three teams, representing the three rotations. The school learned to reserve one of the teams for any parents who spoke only Spanish. This helped eliminate the need for translators in each group. Here are sample sign-in sheets for three rotation groups.

In this example, the three rotation teams were identified by the symbols of a pencil, scissors, and a book. The pencil team followed the pencil rotation schedule. The scissors followed the scissors rotation schedule. The book followed the book rotation schedule. This ensured all parents and their children would rotate to all of the training sessions.

The parents followed a printed schedule. This helped them know where they would be going and for how long. It helped the presenters stay on schedule. It also helped direct parents who were late arrivers to get to the correct location quickly. Here is a sample.

Name/Nombre	Student Name/Nombre del Estudiante	Teacher/Maestra

Name/Nombre	Student Name/Nombre del Estudiante	Teacher/Maestra

Name/Nombre	Student Name/Nombre del Estudiante	Teacher/Maestra

Figure 8.1: Sign-in Sheets

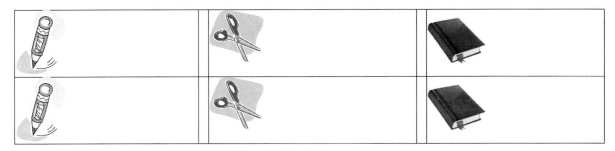

Figure 8.2: Sample Name Tag Stickers to Identify Parent Rotation Group

8:00 – 8:30 Registration 8:30 – 8:45 Welcome Cafeteria	8:00 – 8:30 Registration 8:30 – 8:45 Welcome Cafeteria	8:00 – 8:30 Registration 8:30 – 8:45 Welcome Cafeteria
9:00 – 9:45 Reading Specialist: Reading Resources Library	10:30 – 11:15 Counselor and Nurse: Test Taking Skills & Science Resources Compass Lab ~ Room 102	9:45 – 10:30 Classroom Teachers: Math Resources Sequoyah Lab ~ Room 203
9:45 – 10:30 Classroom Teachers: Math Resources Sequoyah Lab ~ Room 203	9:00 – 9:45 Reading Specialist: Reading Resources Library	10:30 – 11:15 Counselor and Nurse: Test Taking Skills & Science Resources Compass Lab ~ Room 102
10:30 – 11:15 Counselor and Nurse: Test Taking Skills & Science Resources Compass Lab ~ Room 102	9:45 – 10:30 Classroom Teachers: Math Resources Sequoyah Lab ~ Room 203	9:00 – 9:45 Reading Specialist: Reading Resources Library
11:15 – 11:45 Family Game Time Gym	11:15 – 11:45 Family Game Time Gym	11:15 – 11:45 Family Game Time Gym

Figure 8.3: Parent Rotation Chart

SAMPLE PARENT EDUCATION PLANS

The following are sample activities that you can consider using for parent training. These activities can be implemented with minimal preparation on your part. You may be able to find an expert in your area who can provide these kinds of trainings for your patrons. Each sample event follows the same simple template used for parent-child literacy interactions. The template includes:

1. Title
2. Goal for children
3. Goal for parents: What do you want them to *understand*?
4. Approximate time needed
5. Supplies needed
6. Family literacy event description
7. Conclusion: What do you urge the parents to *do* with what they learned from you?

Here are two sample activities from Jefferson Elementary school's counselor, Angela Totman.

TITLE: HIGH SELF ESTEEM + POSITIVE SELF-IMAGE = SCHOOL SUCCESS

Grade levels: Elementary

Submitted by: Angela Totman

Goal for children: To increase student's self-esteem and positive self-image, which in turn increases their success in school (the goal of all educators).

Goal for parents: What do you want them to *understand*? That children need to be raised in a structured, stable environment where rules are consistently enforced and children are consistently praised and rewarded for positive choices. Parents also need to set aside time to interact and spend quality time with their children. Parents should communicate their feelings with their children and encourage their children to share their feelings about situations at school and home with them as well.

Approximate time needed: 45 minutes

Supplies needed: Laptop, Eiki projector, handouts, reward chart.

Family literacy event description

Explain the use of a rewards chart at home. Discuss different things children should be rewarded for. Discuss how praise can help provide positive reinforcement and encourage the repetition of the thing you are rewarding. Possible ideas include:

1. Spend time reading to your child or have your child read to you: discuss your favorite parts of the book and the characters' feelings.
2. Encourage your child to talk to you about school and be a good listener: Be positive. Avoid judgmental or critical comments.
3. Eat healthy meals together as a family: healthy meals stimulate our brain.
4. Exercise together as a family: exercise is a great stress reliever.

In all of these behaviors, parents should be a positive role model for their children. They will imitate what you do and say.

Conclusion: What do you urge the parents to do with what they learned from you?

Apply lessons to your daily life. Though there often isn't a lot of time in our daily lives, we need to make time for our children. Children (and adults) need to spend less time watching TV or playing video games and spend more time interacting with each other. Children often act out in school because they are seeking the attention they are not getting at home. When they are disruptive in class, they are not able to learn. Success in school starts in the home!

TITLE: COPING WITH STRESS

Grade levels: Elementary

Submitted by: Angela Totman

Goal for children: To assist children's success in school, particularly with some of the statewide tests administered to children, such as the TAKS (Texas Assessment of Knowledge and Skills) test, and to teach strategies for coping with stress.

Goal for parents: What do you want them to *understand?* Stress is a natural part of life and some stress can be good when it motivates us to accomplish our goals. Lots of issues can cause stress in children, in addition to the TAKS test. Help your child identify when he/she is stressed and learn to cope with stress effectively through the use of various techniques. Learn test-taking tips to assist your child to be successful in school.

Approximate time needed: 45 minutes

Supplies needed: Laptop, Eiki projector, handouts, test prep cards, bookmarks.

Family literacy event description

1. Learn what stress is and how it can be good or bad: learn what issues may cause stress.
2. Learn the signs of harmful stress: seek professional help immediately if your child shows these signs.
3. Encourage your child to work out a plan to deal with the cause of stress: Discuss the plan afterwards, praise the effort, discuss other ways the problem could have been handled.
4. Teach your child to manage stress using various techniques such as deep breathing, six-second quieting response, progressive muscle relaxation, meditation, imagery, exercise, healthy eating, and getting enough rest.
5. Reinforce the test-taking techniques discussed here with your children.

Conclusion: What do you urge the parents to do with what they learned from you?

Communicate with your children and encourage them to talk to you about anything at school or home that they feel stressed about. Assist your children in working through the stress. Communicate with your children's teachers to find out how they are doing in school. Make sure your children are practicing the test-taking tips discussed. Be a positive role model for your children and always "practice what you preach." Practice coping well with stress yourself and your children will be more likely to cope well, too.

Most public librarians are not reading specialists and should welcome suggestions from any reading specialist in the school district. The reading specialist from Jefferson Elementary shared the following examples of what you may want to address when speaking to parents about "on grade level" reading.

TITLE: FOR THE LOVE OF READING

Grade levels: Kindergarten, first, and second
Submitted by: Diana Morales
Goal for student: Know the importance of reading with fluency and comprehension. Know parents care about their success by participating in the reading experience.
Goal for parents: What do you want them to *understand?* To realize that they are their child's first teachers and an integral part of the relationship between home and school.

Family literacy event description

1. PowerPoint on the importance of reading and how it ties in to all content areas.
2. Making and breaking words.
3. Dolch High Frequency Words for the particular grade level.
4. Reading in phrases to improve fluency.
5. Provide samples of different levels of questions.
6. Ideas as to how to make reading more fun.
7. Urging parents to get a library card and visiting regularly.
8. Take-home activities
   a. alphabet activities
   b. garage door books for beginning, middle, and end
   c. making pop-up books
   d. using shaving cream idea for spelling practice
   e. encourage writing in journals and diaries (These can be made out of a plain spiral that has been decorated any way the child wishes or by adding drawings or gluing photographs of the child.)
9. Accelerated Reading / Enterprise and Star Testing.
10. Include PowerPoint slides on how reading ties in to writing, as well as other areas of the curriculum.
11. Evaluation sheet to be provided at the end of your presentation.

Conclusion: What do you urge parents to do with what they learned from you?

Statistics show that children who are successful readers in first grade will be successful in later years. All content areas require a student to read with comprehension.

Encourage parents to use a few of these ideas at a time. Ask them to revisit the folder they take home and incorporate a few new ones later. Encourage asking questions from the different levels of questioning. Inform them that higher order thinking questions are not just for gifted and talented students. Higher order thinking skills questions encourage all students to think outside the box. Model higher order thinking skills during the presentation. For example, take an empty water bottle and ask the children in the audience what you could do with the bottle after drinking the water. Keep asking, "What else?" Parents witness how students brainstorm ideas and that the students begin to be more creative with their responses. Encourage parents to do this at home; the lesson can be an "aha moment" for them.

CONCLUSION

The goal of this chapter was to help you to see ways you can begin to train the parents and families of the children you serve. What parent would not want the best for their child? The problem is some parents feel ill prepared to help their child, especially in the area of literacy. Darling (2004) said: "One of the primary motivators for families to participate in family literacy programs is parents' desire for their children to succeed. If parents are to be primary teachers of their children, their participation is vital. Family literacy programs may be particularly adept at gaining commitment from parents who are facing multiple barriers to participation in an educational program" (p. 608) If you plan thoughtfully to meet families needs and advertise well, your parents and families will come. They want the best for their child, and you are in a special position to offer them opportunities for both parent-child literacy interactions and parenting education and support.

References

Darling, S. (2004). Future directions for family literacy. In B. H. Wasik (Ed.), *Handbook of family literacy* (pp. 603–616). Mahwah, NJ: Lawrence Erlbaum Associates.

Wasik, B. H. (2004). Family literacy programs: Synthesizing across themes, theories, and recommendations. In B. H. Wasik (Ed.), *Handbook of family literacy* (pp. 617–631). Mahwah, NJ: Lawrence Erlbaum Associates.

CHAPTER 9

What Is Special about Bilingual/ Multicultural Family Literacy?

With contributions from Dr. Maria Magdalena Aguilar Crandall and Dr. John A. Sutterby

When designing a family literacy event for your library, it is important to identify the target audience you want to serve. Often times the target audience includes at-risk or culturally diverse children and families. Staff development may be necessary to train staff and faculty to work with families that are different from their own. This is important since many times these workers are the main players in your family literacy events. They may be unaware of the different issues your target audience faces on a daily basis. Staff and faculty need to see that they are addressing the child's needs by working with the family system. Family systems may not be an area they are familiar with.

Public librarians recognize the importance of promoting literacy to all patrons. However, when serving culturally and linguistically diverse (CLD) children, the librarian may need to make concerted effort to meet their needs. Establishing your library as the hub for information access is vital. Your goals might include connecting these children to information they can understand and help them develop patterns of regular library use. Librarians should be familiar with research surrounding issues related to literacy practices in CLD homes and should be aware of family literacy models developed to address various ethnic groups.

LITERACY PRACTICES IN CULTURALLY AND LINGUISTICALLY DIVERSE HOMES

An overview of Chu and Wu's(2010) study titled *Understanding Literacy Practices in Culturally and Linguistically Diverse (CLD) Children's Homes* reveals several factors influencing home literacy practices surrounding young CLD children. These factors include: opportunities to access literacy materials, amounts of reading materials, bilingual books, book-reading frequency, and degree of parental involvement. Let's examine ways you as a librarian can provide assistance to families that are culturally and linguistically diverse.

Libraries can provide opportunities for families to *access literacy materials* that they do not have in their homes. Public and school librarians should work together to encourage a regular routine of families checking out books. Advertise for each other on your websites. Public libraries can add a parent page to their website that links parents to local public and private school libraries. School libraries can provide links to the local library branch. Public libraries should consider sending membership applications to the school librarians to distribute to families. Public librarians can also visit schools during PTA/PTO meetings and recruit membership.

Depending on where you live, there are other ways for families to access literacy materials. Many local Public Broadcast Service (PBS) television stations offer parent workshops following a make and take format. Contact your local station and see what they offer for parent education. Some use the "Ready to Learn" model, which teaches families how to watch good TV, read a book about a particular subject, and do a hands-on related activity. Some programs even offer free books to the families they train.

You may be familiar with books such as *What to Expect When You Are Expecting* or *What to Expect the First Year*. These books are intriguing to new parents who anxiously read to find out what exciting thing will happen in their baby's life this month or this year. They read to see if their child is "on track" and doing what is "developmentally appropriate." Sadly, there are few if any similar choices of reading materials describing children as they grow up. What if you could offer families details of the stages of literacy their child will experience each year.

The Reading Foundation's website (http://www.readingfoundation.org/parents/schoolage.jsp) details information concerning several grade levels. Take this kind of information from reputable sources recognized by your district or state. Work with others to develop items to share with families. Consider using a newsletter or brochure, parent workshops, bookmarks, parent webpage(s), and home literacy bags.

Chu and Wu's (2010) study also recognized the importance of *amounts of reading materials* available in the home. As a librarian, there are many ways to help families in this area. As mentioned earlier, encouraging visits to the library is important. Libraries provide almost limitless access to books for families. The Harlingen, Texas, public library has found an excellent way to promote their library use. The patrons receive a slip of paper listing their checked-out books and then includes an estimated cost of what it would have cost if the patron had purchased the books. For example, the slip states: "You have saved $65.34 today."

Among the other ways to increase the amounts of reading materials available in the home of culturally and linguistically diverse families, public librarians could urge school librarians to consider extending their library hours to accommodate families. Many parents who walk their children to school would welcome an opportunity to get books there rather than to have to arrange transportation to the public library. You have to know your population well to know their needs and schedule. Many school libraries are beginning to extend their library hours to accommodate open library times before and after the school day. Some school libraries are opening during the summer to help prevent summer reading loss. Public libraries are planning programs that take place after school hours and during school vacation times. Another strategy, along

As a kindergartner, your child:

- Begins to see him or herself as a reader
- Understands that print goes from left to right and has meaning

Left -→ Right

- Can say letters and point to letters of the alphabet
  A B C D E F G H I J K L M N O P Q R S T U V W X Y Z

- Knows all the consonant sounds and may know the vowel sounds
- Recognizes simple words like "the," "and," "it," and "is"
- Starts to read signs, food packages, and other everyday items
- Likes being read to and has favorite books and stories
- Produces rhyming words **Cat - Hat**
- Can write his or her own name

http://www.readingfoundation.org/parents/schoolage.jsp

Figure 9.1: Kindergarten Parent Bookmark (Front and Back of Bookmark) a different line of thinking, is teaching parents how to turn on the closed captioning component of their home TV. Students would have live reading materials racing in front of their eyes s they follow the conversations of their favorite TV programs. They will potentially begin to recognize more words and see their definitions played out in context.

Bilingual books should be available in all libraries given the changing demographics in the United States. Having these books suggests that libraries recognize and value diversity in cultures and languages. Bilingual books are also a tool to increase all of your patrons' awareness of the diversity that surrounds them. Ask publishers about books published in specific dialects to serve your patrons.

Be aware of the different formats available for bilingual books. Think about the age of your patrons to help you choose the right format. Possible formats include:

1. Books published in different versions for each language. These are published as separate books. For example, one book is in English and the same title is published in Spanish or Mandarin.
2. Books with complete text in two languages. Sometimes these books show one language on the right side of a double-spread page with matching text in another language on the left side of the page. The same could be done with the top and bottom of a single- or double-spread page.
3. Books that switch between languages. For example, the book may be written in English with some character's lines written in another language.
4. Books written in English intermingled with words or phrases in another language. This is sometimes referred to as "code switching," where there is concurrent use of more than one language scattered throughout the text.

The Chu and Wu (2010) study also mentions the significance of *book-reading frequency*. This ties in directly to a child's fluency. Reading fluency is typified by smooth and quick reading, which allows the reader to focus on comprehension instead of the act of reading itself. Some problems are associated with poor fluency. Children

| | | | | | | 's Fluency Bookmark |
Monday	Tuesday	Wednesday	Thursday	Friday	Saturday	Sunday
Count the words you read in one minute. Write it in the box. You should get faster by the end of the week.						
Words per minute	1st grade 50–70	2nd grade 70–100	3rd grade 100–130	4th grade 130–140	5th grade 140–160	6th grade 160–170

Figure 9.2: Bookmark for Home Fluency Practice
Source: Words per Minute taken from Reading A–Z (2011).

who are poor readers may yet know how to decode well, may decode well but read haltingly, or may even be a laborious and slow process.

Help parents realize the value of repeated readings and the need for their child to read often. Send home a simple book mark that will allow them to work on fluency by encouraging repeated readings and showing their child how practice leads to improvement in words read per minute. Let parents know there is value in both reading to their child and listening to their child read to them.

Finally, the *degree of parental involvement* makes a difference in CLD children's literacy. Most people would agree that parental involvement makes a difference in all children's lives, not just the CLD children. Librarians and educators want parents to talk with their children about what they are reading. We want them to model reading at home. However, many parents are too busy to read the books themselves or too busy to figure out what to ask. Give parents an easy way to get involved.

Take a hint from some of the trendy dinner table boxed activity sets. These boxed sets have individual cards a family can pull out and use as the dinner table discussion topic for the evening. Dr. Teri Lesesne (2003) encourages librarians and reading teachers to use questions created by author Richard Peck (1978) to guide purposeful discussions with children. These questions could easily be crafted on to index cards or a similar medium to use around the dinner table. Parents who had not read the books their children were reading are able to have an interesting and deeper level of conversation about their children's choice of reading materials.

_____'s Parent Library Homework							
	Monday	Tuesday	Wednesday	Thursday	Friday	Saturday	Sunday
I read to my family							
My family reads to me							

Figure 9.3: Bookmark for Home Fluency Practice

Table 9.1 Richard Peck Questions

1. What would this story be like if the main character were of the opposite sex?
2. Why is this story set where it is (not what is the setting)?
3. If you were to film this story, what characters would you eliminate if you couldn't use them all?
4. Would you film this story in black and white or in color?
5. How is the main character different from you?
6. Why would or wouldn't this story make a good TV series?
7. What's one thing in this story that's happened to you?
8. Reread the first paragraph of chapter 1. What's in it that makes you read on?
9. If you had to design a new cover for this book, what would it look like?
10. What does the title tell you about the book? Does it tell the truth?

FAMILY LITERACY MODELS FROM THE AMERICAN LIBRARY ASSOCIATION'S FIVE ETHNIC AFFILIATES

Thanks in part to the American Library Association (ALA) and Dr. Camila Alire, past president of the ALA, you have access to a variety of resources when creating events to serve your diverse populations. During the 2009–2010 year, ALA awarded money to the five ethnic affiliates to create a family literacy model to encourage their families to read and learn together. These subgroups included libraries serving African Americans, Asian and Pacific Americans, Chinese Americans, Latino Americans, and Native Americans. The leaders from the ethnic affiliate unveiled their creations at ALA's annual conference in June 2010. These models were intended to be easily replicable and available for free to the public via the Internet. These models were developed by the affiliates who are intimately aware of the culture and traditions of their respective group. During the ALA conference, the groups also mentioned the activities in each model can be used by any group of people. They also encouraged librarians to think these plans were not only for intact families, but also adoptive families who may have children from other cultures.

The Black Caucus of the American Library Association (BCALA, 2010) developed a family literacy program titled Reading is Grand! This program was designed to celebrate the important role grandparents play in the lives of children. Grandparents are recognized as the ones often serving as primary caregivers. This project provides opportunities for them to build literacy in their grandchildren's lives through shared stories.

Reading is Grand! encouraged the shared reading of new stories, the telling of old stories, and writing family books together. The telling of personal stories allows the older generation to pass down values and stories from their own childhood. Creating a book of this story solidifies the relationship between the generations and creates a memory keepsake for years to come. The website also provides a list of books that portray extended families and honor of grandparents (BCALA, 2010).

Talk Story: Sharing Stories, Sharing Culture was developed to serve Asian Pacific American (APA) and American Indian/Alaska Native (AIAN) children and their families (Asian Pacific American [APA] and American Indian/Alaska Native [AIAN], 2010). This family literacy program uses books, oral traditions, and art to celebrate and explore APA and AIAN cultural stories. While Talk Story was designed for use in homes, libraries, and communities, it can easily be modified for all ethnicities. It was piloted in three Asian Pacific American Library Association (APALA) libraries: the Carson Regional Library, Carson, California; the Queens Library, Flushing, New York; and the Loren Corey Eiseley Branch Library, Lincoln, Nebraska; and three American Indian Library Association (AILA) libraries: Laguna Public Library, Laguna, New Mexico; Jemez Community Pueblo Library, Jemez, New Mexico; and Tuzzy Consortium Library, Barrow, Alaska.

The Talk Story website includes a bibliography of books about the AIAN and APA experiences. Their website offers a multitude of story time ideas and a template for you use when developing own events. Their story time ideas include topics such as adoption and multicultural families, origami story time, and woodlands native American harvest festival. Each topic includes an opening idea, multiple book choices, activities, and a closing activity. At the time of this writing, they welcome outside submissions of similar events that fit their theme; and they also sponsor a competitive grant to fund others who implement their program.

Dai Dai Xiang Chuan was developed by ALA's Chinese American Librarians Association (CALA, 2010) to bring generations together through culture, reading, movement, and technology. Their project is titled Dai Dai Xiang Chuan: Bridging Generations, a Bag at a Time. They produced a Chinese pun using a single word with a double meaning. Dai means "bag" and "passing on information from one generation to another." CALA worked with four libraries around the United States to create 20 themed bags that contained books, games, audiovisual materials, and other items along with instructions in both English and Chinese. The participating libraries included: the Cleveland Public Library (Ohio), Miami University Libraries and Talawanda (Ohio) School District, the Middlebury (Indiana) Community Public Library, and the San Francisco (California) Public Library–Visitacion Valley.

These bags were available for checkout by the target audience. A blog was developed for participants to share their experiences using the bags and for the libraries to work together on this project implementation. The idea was for the bags to provide opportunities for generations within families to interact together around some kind of literacy activity. A resource list was developed for project participants but will also be useful to anyone trying to replicate the project.

REFORMA: The National Association to Promote Library and Information Services to Latinos and the Spanish Speaking developed a family literacy program called Noche de Cuentos/A Night of Stories (REFORMA, 2010). This program focused on storytelling and oral traditions to promote oral literacy and consequently unite and strengthen their culture. Five libraries participated in the original implementation of Noche de Cuentos: Charlotte Mecklenburg Public Library (North Carolina), the Half Moon Bay Branch, San Mateo County Public Library (California), Mexican American Cultural Center and El Corazon de Tejas REFORMA Chapter (Texas), National City Public Library and Libros REFORMA Chapter (California), and Salinas Public Library (California).

This program was designed as a one night event where Latino families joined the global community in celebrating World Storytelling Day at their local libraries. World Storytelling Day is celebrated every year in the northern hemisphere on the spring equinox and in the southern hemisphere on the first day of the autumn equinox. The goal is to have as many people as possible, using as many languages as possible, tell and listen to stories on the same date.

The following section is written by Drs. Maria Magdalena Aguilar Crandall and John A. Sutterby. Their experiences working with Spanish-speaking and bilingual children and families in South Texas has afforded them practical experience for working with multicultural families.

ADAPTING LIBRARIES FOR MULTILINGUAL/ MULTICULTURAL POPULATIONS

In *Tomas and the Library Lady,* Pat Mora describes Tomás Riveras's experiences as a child as a migrant farm worker traveling from Texas to Iowa with his family. In Iowa, Tomás visits a library and is taken under the wing of the local librarian. He also has strong ties to the oral tradition of his family. Tomás Rivera later grew up to be an academic scholar, writer, and college president of the University of California, Riverside. The story describes how librarians can have an impact on children from backgrounds of differences in language and culture. It also describes how these differences can be bridged by people who care.

Increases in Multicultural/Multilingual Population

According to the American Library Association (2008), libraries have to adapt to the needs of non-English–speaking patrons. About 21 million U.S. residents speak little or no English. Spanish is by far the language most commonly spoken other than English; with Hmong, Vietnamese, and Chinese being the other most common languages. Surprisingly, the libraries that are facing the highest demand for non-English materials and services are in smaller communities rather than large urban communities.

School librarians also have to adapt to these demographic changes. In 2005 the number of English language learners (ELL) in schools was more than 5.3 million, which is about 10% of the U.S. school-age population. The states with the highest concentration of ELLs are Arizona, California, Texas, Florida, New York, North Carolina, and Illinois. The states with the fastest growth rates, as high as 300%, are Alabama, Indiana, Kentucky, Colorado, Virginia, Georgia, Arkansas, North Carolina, South Carolina, and Tennessee (National Clearinghouse for English Language Acquisition [NCELA], 2011). This demographic shift leads to many challenges for librarians who have not traditionally had to develop services for non-English–speaking populations.

Multicultural Expectations

Librarians who are experiencing demographic changes in their library populations need to get to know and understand these changes in order to better serve their population. As Mississippi Byrd writes, "the most important ingredient in building Latino participation is willingness" (2000, p. 1.). This applies to all language and cultural expectations. According to Vang (2004), Hmong library patrons most often use library services for survival information like English language classes. Vang suggests that most Hmong do not use library services because they use family and ethnic connections to gather information. Because many Hmong do not read either English or their own language, it is important for libraries to reach out to this population, especially in nontraditional ways. Willingness goes a long way to opening libraries to different populations. Willingness means getting to know the local population, their understanding of libraries, and being willing to develop services that meet their needs and find texts in languages other than English.

One area that librarians will need to understand is how different groups view libraries. For example, librarians will need to be aware that different cultures will have different expectations on things like greeting, welcoming, and time management. Different cultures may also have different ways of passing on news and information that bypass traditional methods like newspapers and advertisements.

Librarians should try to become familiar with some elements of the culture in order to avoid confusion. Getting to know cultures can be done through different means. An indirect way to get to know a specific culture is to approach someone who has worked closely with a group of parents or with a specific community. Individuals who have worked closely with parents who are part of the a particular cultural community can be a great source of information in reference to cultural nuances. A direct way to get to know a specific culture is to become familiar with someone within the culture. Once they have achieved a level of comfort, they can politely request assistance in the correct manners in relation to approaching a group of people within the community.

While becoming aware of the patrons' culture, librarians should also try and get to know the patron's experiences with the library system of their country of origin. While some children may be familiar with library policies on lending books, other children (and their parents) may not comprehend the possibility of so many materials available to patrons free for the borrowing. Some Latino children and their families emigrate from areas where access to libraries (whether public libraries or school libraries) has been minimal to nonexistent (Moller, 2001). Some children have attended schools where a library building was part of the campus; however, it was not functioning as a library. And other children have attended schools where there was no library at all. Mexico's history and experiences with children's libraries is relatively new. Many librarians and scholars in Mexico agree that the 1970s produced the first serious endeavor to provide children with access to libraries (Schon, 2009). This effort to provide libraries for children still has a long way to go.

Alternative Literacies

Some cultures will place different priorities on what they will see as literacy materials. For example, in Mexico there is more of an emphasis on comic books and magazines rather than on children's literature. So stocking comic books and magazines in Spanish in a school with a high Mexican immigrant population would be helpful. Other groups, for example some religious groups, see reading for pleasure as a waste of time and will only read nonfiction or religious texts. They may be resistant to allowing their children to read fiction.

Many immigrant communities have newspapers available in their native language. Having these available in your library might attract parents. They are often free. These can be helpful in reaching communities like Mandarin-, Arabic-, or Farsi-reading communities who read using a different alphabet.

Access to computers is one area that attracts parents to libraries. Children are now expected to be able to conduct research online. Parents also may be interested in being able to access computer information. One way to attract parents to libraries would be by teaching them how to use computers and then allowing them to access the library's computers. It could be advertised as a way to link to their home countries. In addition, advances in translation software have made online translation more seamless for many languages. Getting parents into the library will help them learn about all the information available in the library.

When children enter school, they are taught how to use computers and they are encouraged to use classroom and library computers for school work and research. While children may begin to become familiar with the use of computers and the Internet, their parents may not have the opportunity to develop their computers and searching skills in comparison to their own children's capabilities. Librarians can make a great connection with parents if they take the time to meet with parents and show them the type of computer, Internet, and research knowledge that is expected of children in U.S. schools. Parents who still have families in foreign countries can be taught to keep in contact with them via the Internet. Provide parents with the skills to open communication lines through free services such as the Internet, Skype, and other social medias. Meetings with parents can be set up during the school day, after school, or on the weekends, depending on the needs of the community and on the availability of the librarian.

Outreach to Populations with Low Technology Experiences

Although many recent immigrants come to the United States with an understanding of technology, there are different levels of experiences with technology. Some immigrants to the United States have had little to no access to technology. For example, within the large Somali populations who have come to the United States, many do not have any literacy skills, even in their home language. Hmong immigrants to the United States, primarily from Cambodia, also have more of an oral tradition. This might make life difficult for the librarian. Librarians can help these populations' understandings of the alphabet as well as developing oral language by providing story times, which can be conducted by people who can tell stories.

School libraries are uncommon in many developing countries like Mexico, Somalia, and Vietnam. Outreach is important in that some immigrant parents do not understand how U.S. libraries work and may not want their children to check out books because they think there might be a charge or they are afraid that they will have to pay for the book if something happens to it. This is also partially an economic issue. In many Latin American countries and in Mexico, books are very expensive so most children are limited to reading their textbooks.

Librarians need to help their patrons understand the level of confidentiality that is upheld by librarians. Patrons not familiar with library ethics may not comprehend that information provided or retrieved by patrons, while using library materials, will be confidential. You and your public librarian colleagues may need to explain to patrons, and their parents, that the books they check out and the information researched at the library will not be released to any type of governmental offices. This is especially important for undocumented parents and children who may see applying for a library card as a risk leading to possible deportation.

School librarians commonly distribute library news through handouts, newsletters, e-mails, and school announcements. All too often these methods of circulating information may not be very effective with families who are from different cultures. Language may be a barrier for some parents. Therefore, handouts, newsletters, e-mails, and even school announcements (including those done at the end of the day) need to be done in the language of non-English speakers. You may need to help your school librarian counterparts to consider other ways to disseminate library information, especially when parent meetings will be held. Some non-English–speaking parents may not be literate or may originate from an oral-dominant background. In such cases, librarians need to consider media other than the written word. Whether it is through local television or radio stations running public announcements, community service organizations, or a local church, librarians should contemplate using various means of connecting with parents.

Selecting Literature

Many organizations exist that are dedicated to improving library services for Hispanic children. REFORMA (http://www.reforma.org) is the national organization dedicated to improving library services for Latinos and Spanish speakers in the United States. They are affiliated with the American Library Association. The Trejo Foster Foundation (http://www.tffoundation.org) provides professional development opportunities for librarians wanting to know more about serving Hispanic/Latino and Spanish-speaking communities. The APALA promotes improving libraries to meet the needs of Asian Americans and Pacific Islanders.

Awards for Literature

One way of finding children's books that are high in quality is to look for books that have won literary awards. Once librarians have familiarized themselves with these award-winning books, they can then promote them to children and their parents. These books can be presented to all children who use the library. Presentations can be scheduled to promote award-winning books to parents in general or specifically to parents of the specific culture you are targeting. Three main book awards for books emphasize Latino culture: the Pura Belpré Award, the Tomás Rivera Award, and the Americas Award. There are also awards for Asian American literature.

The Pura Belpré Award focuses on books from the United States that cover topics from Latin American authors and illustrators. This award is given to books that affirm Latin American culture. This award is given by REFORMA and the Association of Library Services to Children. Pura Belpré award winners include Pam Muñoz Ryan (2010) for *The Dreamer* and Victor Martinez (2004) for *Parrot in the Oven: Mi Vida*.

The Tomás Rivera award is awarded to Mexican American authors and illustrators. The Tomás Rivera award is awarded through Texas State University. Award winners include Pat Mora (2002) for *A Library for Juana* and Carmen Lomas Garza (2000) for *In My Family*.

The Americas Award covers Latin American and Caribbean authors and illustrators. This award is awarded by the Consortium of Latin American Studies Programs (CLASP). This award goes to children's books that authentically represent portrayals of Latin American, Caribbean, and Latinos in the United States.

The APALA awards books by authors and illustrators who represent the Asian American heritage. For example *Roots and Wings* by Ly May (2008) describes the experiences of a Cambodian girl adapting to U.S. culture.

Translations and Bilingual Texts

Many books will have either the English and Spanish text, or text in another language. However, librarians need to take caution when selecting books that are either bilingual or a translation from English to Spanish or other languages. Some translations have Spanish text that has been translated literally, which produces poor grammar and inappropriate phrases or sentences, which then leads to a poor representation of the Spanish language (Schon, 2009). One example of this is *The Phantom Tollbooth* by Norten Juster (1961), which is available in a Spanish edition *La Caseta Majica*. The many puns and inside jokes in English do not make any sense in Spanish. A "watch dog" and a "spelling bee" do not translate from one language to the next. The reader may understand the basic plot story while missing the clever puns of the text.

Librarians must be vigilant while making selections for their collection development. Selection of books that show a wide range of economic conditions is necessary to correctly embody the Latino (or any other)community. Not all English language learners are farm workers, poor, and/or uneducated. Librarians must be selective in how Latinos are represented in the books purchased for the library. For example, Gary Soto's (1993) *Too Many Tamales* represents images of middle-class Mexican American culture.

Children in the Middle

Most immigrant parents are interested in having their children succeed in the American culture while at the same time staying connected to the culture of the country from which they originate. Children may be stuck in the middle. The child may understand the American culture better than their parents yet must continue to show respect. Books that represent such life experiences can help children obtain a sense of validation in the knowledge that they are not the only ones living these experiences. Children (and librarians) can use these books to show their parents the experiences felt by those stuck between two cultures. Books such as *The Tequila Worm* by Viola Canales (2005) and *Breaking Through* by Franciso Jimenez (2001) show such stories of children caught between the Americanization of their characters while being pulled by parents who do not want their children to lose their *cultura*. The book *A Step from Heaven* by An Na (2001) describes how a Korean girl has to find balance between her American culture and the culture of her family. She has to balance respect for her father while being required to act as translator for him on official business. This puts her and her father in the awkward position of her being the source of information for him.

Librarians may sometimes communicate with parents while using the child as an interpreter. One must remember that when the child is the one doing the translation, the parent is still the decision maker in the family so while a librarian may be tempted to direct the conversation to the child, they must keep in mind to focus on the parent and have the conversation with the parent. Issues may arise when parents do not understand the American library system and will not be willing to use the services due to the lack of understanding of how the system works. At the same time, their child may have a better understanding of the American library system and will be more willing to use the services but may have to defer to the parent's decisions whether they agree with them or not. Librarians must remain respectful of the parent's authority.

Closing Thoughts

Librarians play an important role in helping their patrons gather information. Librarians need to adapt to the demographic changes occurring across the United States. In order to meet the needs of their community, librarians need to understand the different linguistic and cultural groups in their community. In serving the community, they need to understand how library services like story time, alternative literacies, and quality literature can impact non-English–speaking and diverse families. Librarians can also help bridge the gap faced by many children when they grow up with one foot in the United States and the other in another country.

CONCLUSION

When trying to make connections to culturally and linguistically diverse families, it is vital to consider some key things about your library and its holdings. Parents and their children will not be interested in visiting your library or attending programs you offer if they do not believe you have items in your collection specifically for them.

Find ways to showcase the areas of your collection that represent diverse cultures, languages, and ethnicities. Be sure to have bilingual or foreign language material suitable for your patrons. Also, be sure to have professional materials for your teachers and community members who work the most with these families. When these families see that you are making strides to serve them and reach out to them, they will be more willing to check out the programming you offer.

References

American Indian Library Association and Asian/Pacific American Libraries Association. (2010). *Talk story: Sharing stories, sharing culture.* Retrieved from http://www.talkstorytogether.org/.

American Library Association. (2008). *Serving non-English speakers in U.S. public libraries: 2007 analysis of library demographics, services and programs.* Chicago, IL: Author.

Black Caucus of the American Library Association. (2010). *BCALA ALA family literacy focus.* Retrieved from http://www.bcala.org/Family%20Literacy/Family%20Literacy.htm.

Canales, V. (2005). *The tequila worm.* New York: Wendy Lamb Books.

Chinese American Librarians Association. (2010). *Dai dai xiang chuan: ALA-CALA family literacy project.* Retrieved from http://daidai.cala-web.org/.

Chu, S.Y., & Wu, H.P. (2010). Understanding literacy practices in culturally and linguistically diverse children's homes. *New Horizons for Learning, 8*(2). Retrieved from http://education.jhu.edu/newhorizons/Journals/Fall2010/Chu-Wu.

Jimenez, F. (2001). *Breaking through.* Boston: Houghton Mifflin Books.

Juster, N. (1961). *The phantom tollbooth.* New York: Random House.

Lesesne, T.S. (2003). *Making the match: The right book for the right reader at the right time.* Portland, ME: Stenhouse Publishers.

Lomas Garza, C. (2000). *In my family/En mi Familia.* San Francisco: Children's Book Press.

Ly, M. (2008). *Roots and wings.* New York: Delacorte.

Martinez, V. (2004). *Parrot in the oven: Mi Vida.* New York: Rayo.

Mississippi Byrd, S. (2000). *Bienvenidos, Welcome: A handy resource guide for marketing your library to Latinos.* Chicago, IL: American Library Association.

Moller, S. (2001). *Library service to Spanish speaking patrons: A practical guide.* Englewood, CO: Libraries Unlimited.

Mora, P. (1997). *Tomas and the library lady.* New York: Random House.

Mora, P. (2002). *A library for Juana.* New York: Knopf Books.

Muñoz Ryan, P. (2010). *The Dreamer.* New York: Scholastic Press.

Na, A. (2001). *A step from heaven.* New York: Speak.

National Clearinghouse for English Language Acquisition. (2011). *The growing number of English Language Learners 1998/1999–2008/2009.* Retrieved from http://www.ncela.gwu.edu/files/uploads/9/growingLEP_0809.pdf.

Peck, R. (1978). Question to ask about a novel. *The ALAN Review,* Spring, 1978, p. 17.

Reading A-Z. (2011). *Fluency.* Retrieved from http://www.readinga-z.com/.

REFORMA. (2010). *Noche de cuentos*. Retrieved from http://nochedecuentos.wordpress.com/.

Schon, I. (2009). *My life: From Mexico City to Arizona to California to San Diego.* Retrieved from http://supportmylibrary.org/pub/My_Life_From_Mexico_City_to_AZ_to_CA_Isabel_Schon2.pdf.

Soto, G. (1993). *Too many tamales*. New York: G.P. Putnam's Sons.

Vang, V. (2004). Public library services to the Hmong-American community: Much room for improvement. *Libres, 14*(1). Retrieved from http://libres.curtin.edu.au/libres14n1/March%2004_Ess%20&%20Op_VangNov20_03.htm.

CHAPTER 10

What Are Special Issues at Family Literacy Events?

As with many things in your professional and personal life, organization is the key to success. Consider the fact that some organizations hire special event organizers to oversee the planning and execution of their events. You will not have that luxury, but you must give as much attention to the planning of your family literacy event as an event organizer would. Careful pre-planning will lead to a smoother event and can prevent many common issues that could arise at an event. If you have carefully thought out your response to common problems, you are well on your way to a successful event. Based on Sheneman's (2010) survey, there are some common issues that can occur at family literacy events. This chapter will address the most often noted issues from the survey.

You must know your audience. Many variables are associated with different types of audiences. For example, if your audience contains an immigrant population, their primary language must be considered. If you are targeting parents of preschool and younger children, child care issues must be addressed. If your audience is older children, what will you do with the younger siblings who have been brought along? Underplanning for the size of audience can be awkward and embarrassing.

We're Beginning
to Sprout!
Come help us grow.

Empezamosa retoñar!
Vengan ayudarnos a crecer.

Figure 10.1: Front of Sample Flyer

PRIMARY LANGUAGE

The audience's primary language should be considered from the early planning stages. Be sure you advertise and recruit in the languages most readily used by your target audience. If you are having someone call the families you are targeting, make certain they are comfortable speaking the language of the families they are calling. Your flyers should be written and distributed in multiple languages, for example the front in English and the back in Spanish or a side-by-side presentation with Spanish on the right side and English on the left. First create your flyer in English, or your dominant language, and have a trusted volunteer (a teacher, translator, close friend, community member, etc.) translate it for you. Be sure to have a second volunteer look it over for clarity.

On the day of the event, you will need to address all the languages present in the audience. Sheneman's (2010) survey respondents described this in several ways. Some used an interpreter who stood in front with the main speaker. The interpreter repeated to the entire audience what the speaker said after each main point. Some even went as far as having a PowerPoint presentation in both languages as well. Others reported having a person sitting close by a single, non-English speaking family to quietly interpret the message for the family group. Others reported they split the group in to smaller sections based on language preference.

PRESCHOOL AND YOUNGER CHILDREN

This age group of children is potentially your target group of children. If you need them with their parents because the parents will be practicing a skill with their child, you must preplan something for them to do as they wait. Possibly you have a small play area where they can be supervised during the adults' direct instruction time. The supervisor could walk the children back at the appropriate time to interact with their parents. If they are older preschool children, you might consider laying out small activities or snacks to entertain the children while the adults are receiving instruction. These items could be coloring sheets, simple puzzles, play dough, or other such items.

However, there are times when the younger children are not the focus of the group. When this is the case, you should consider having child care onsite. By advertising and providing this kind of care, you are showing the families you are aware of their needs and you have put a lot of thought in to your preparations. Providing light refreshments in the child care room can be a big draw to some children. Do what you can to draw them in to the friendly and fun child care you have arranged. Plan a special event or activity just for them.

Sometimes parents are not willing to drop their child off at child care. If this happens, allow them to stay but gently tell the parents that if their child makes it difficult

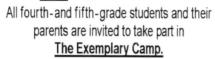

All fourth-and fifth-grade students and their parents are invited to take part in
The Exemplary Camp.

*In order to participate, all students must be accompanied by an adult family member.

Date: Thursday, February 11, 2010
8:30 a.m. – 12:00 p.m.

Any questions?
Contact: Mrs. Librarian at 555-5555

*Please **register** in the cafeteria between
8:15 a.m. – 8:30 a.m.
Sweet bread and coffee will be provided.

* Must be present by 9:00 a.m. to receive pizza ticket.

Todos los estudiantes de 4° y 5° grado y sus padres están invitados a compartir en el
Campo Ejemplar.

*Para participar, los estudiantes deben venir acompañados de un miembro adulto
de la familia.

Fecha: jueves, 11 de febrero, 2010
8:30 a.m. – 12:00 p.m.

¿Tiene preguntas?
Comuníquese con la
Señora Librarian al 555-5555

*Favor de **registrarse** en la cafetería
8:15 a.m. – 8:30 a.m.
donde habrá pan dulce y café.

* Necesita estar presente a las 9:00 a.m. para
recibir un boleto para pizza.

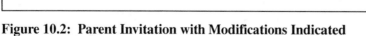

Child Care Provided ~ Room 104
Guardería Infantil ~ Salón 104

Figure 10.2: Parent Invitation with Modifications Indicated

for others to hear, they will need to step out and take them to the child care room. Many young children are able to stay quietly with their parents. However, we have all been in a room when a rambunctious or vocal child has made it difficult to participate in the event. By planning ahead for child care, you will have options for families to do what is best for their particular child.

SIZE OF AUDIENCE

Large audience sizes can be both a blessing and a curse. They are blessings when you have a wonderful event planned and you have all the necessary materials readily at hand. However, underplanning puts you in an uncomfortable position. One school reported they assigned a "runner" to each activity. This runner was ready to make extra copies, dash to the storeroom for more supplies, take a distracting child to child care, and basically take care of any other need that reared its head while the presenter was presenting. Be sure the "runner" is added to your planning sheet. Having someone on call and ready is imperative.

Other organizations noticed the size of their crowd grew larger the closer it got to refreshments or prize time. Another reported they found some parents missed out on the training provided but would show up just in time for the lunch or refreshment period. They solved this concern by publicizing refreshment tickets would be issued during the first 30 minutes of sign-in. These tickets were then collected during the time refreshments were served. A similar solution would work for raffles or door prizes. An "on time" door prize is a fun way to encourage prompt arrivals. Issuing prize tickets to those present at key times would encourage attendance throughout the event.

The following is an actual sample invitation from a school family literacy event. The invitation addresses many of the issues just mentioned. Careful thought went in to the initial invitation. As issues occurred the invitation was modified to address the concern at hand. The stars ★ indicate changes or modifications made to the invitation over time.

CROWD CONTROL

When working with families, you must still view yourself as the leader/teacher. There are times you will need to regroup your audience if they are unfocused or noisy. Just as in good classroom teaching or good presentation techniques, keeping your audience focused is the best way to prevent disruptions. Remember to plan for a variety of activities. Have them sit and stand at different times. Have them form small groups or larger groups, and work alone. Have attractive visual aids. Change your voice tone and volume during the presentation.

Most important of all, make sure your presentation has some component of participation. "I hear, and I forget. I see, and I remember. I do, and I understand." Many old adages have a similar theme, but do your best to incorporate the principles they refer to. You are presenting something to your audience that you consider has value. They are there to listen and learn from you. Build on what they hear. Show them visual aids to demonstrate the main points you are making. Then, get them involved. Have the families practice while you are there in the room. Initially, guide them through what you want them to do. Eventually, leave them on their own to practice their new skill.

CONCLUSION

As with many things in life, planning ahead is vital. Work with your family literacy team to develop a planning sheet. Careful pre-planning will prevent many awkward mistakes. Check in advance with the presenters to be sure they have planned for the size of crowd you anticipate. Remember also to regroup as a team to discuss the problems you encountered. Brainstorm possible solutions. If appropriate, add the solution to your planning guide to ensure your team has the issue covered for your next event. All of this should lead to successful family literacy programming. "Modify and adjust" should be an ongoing mantra as you carry out your family literacy events.

Reference

Sheneman, L. C. (2010). *Family literacy survey*. Retrieved from http://www.surveymonkey. com/sr.aspx?sm=cftN8zqu4WaOWxS9d97RUbQQhpd1iNcJo4Ju2_2b8jxm0_3d.

APPENDIX

Family Literacy Interviews and Reflections

FAMILY LITERACY PUBLIC LIBRARIAN INTERVIEW

Name: Nicki Stohr

1. **How do you define Family Literacy?** Family literacy to us is a service to encourage a family to make sustainable change within the family lifestyle to include reading as an important "family" activity. We are encouraging families as a whole unit to read together.
2. **What caused you to pursue family literacy events for your library? Please include how long you have participated in providing these events and what age students you serve.** We noticed that within our calendar of events we offered only preschool story times and lap sit story times with occasional teen or tween events. So, for the first time, in January 2011, we offered a Winter Family Reading Club modeled after our Summer Reading Club. Each Saturday for six weeks we

expanded our programming calendar to include a 10 A.M. story time. This story time was designed to include all ages, and parental involvement was expected. We had multigenerational story times along with the expected parent-child combination.

3. **What results have you seen at your library that you attribute to hosting family literacy events?** We have been asked to include the same family story time during the summer.

4. **Were there any surprising results, positive or negative, that you did not expect?** The biggest surprise was to see and hear the families were actually changing their Saturday routines to make the library a pit stop on their busy list of things to do.

5. **Were there any difficulties related to these events that you had to work around?** Difficulties included staffing. We learned that those attending on a regular basis were expecting to see the same staff member. It is extremely hard on a small staff like ours to have one individual work every weekend. We do not have the money to expand our staff, so we are trying to introduce a rotating schedule of some kind to accommodate all of our work schedules.

6. **What kind of feedback have you had?** The feedback was generally good. We managed to get our events into the county newspaper each week, and we have been asked to repeat the family model into the Summer Reading Program.

7. **What is the basic format of your events?** Each family event started with a "get to know you" song, read alouds, and book talks; followed by an activity that every family member can participate in. Outside of the Saturday family story time we offered individuals and families a chance to register and log their minutes of reading. We had 65 people logging in for 43,000 minutes of reading in six weeks. This was not bad for a first try! As an added incentive, we offered the participants entries into a drawing for themed baskets that were made to appeal to the whole family. It was similar to a raffle with each entry costing 110 minutes of reading time. The drawing took place after the six-week period.

8. **Who are the key players in your events? Please include the title of their regular position and the role they play in the events.** We are thankful to have a full-time employee who loves to plan and perform story times. Their position is part children's aid and part circulation desk.

9. **How do you pay for these events?** The Family Winter Reading Club was paid for from leftover Summer Reading Club monies. The total cost for our six-week program was approximately $500.

10. **If you were able to speak to other public librarians who are considering beginning their own family literacy events, what words of advice would you have for them?** Advertise your event. Find media to get the word out. Send flyers to school libraries, day cares, and restaurants. We found a way to make the registration process easier by going online and arranging for the first reading time log to be printable from this online process.

FAMILY LITERACY PRINCIPAL INTERVIEW

Name: Manuel Olivo

1. **How do you define Family Literacy?** We have to keep in mind our clientele, the parents. Our clientele here are lacking in a lot of areas. They can't give any help for things they don't have themselves. Family Literacy is when we turn the family on to reading and learning and school. School and reading and learning become part of the vocabulary and that's how we're going to change the neighborhoods around here. It's a change in mentalities. Yes, we need to be concerned about income and this and that, but somehow if we can turn them to at least think about at least once in a while about reading, school, and education, I think then we'll start seeing a change in the neighborhoods. I keep telling people you've really got to start spending money now on the kids at this age (elementary) because once they become gangbangers, it's really hard to get them out. You get them out now by providing what I dream about—that one day Jefferson will be open until at least 8:00 P.M. for kids to come and use the library, do Accelerated Reading, read books, and families can come and do the same thing. That's when we're going to see graffiti go down and things like that.

2. **What caused you to pursue family literacy events for your school? Please include how long you have participated in providing these events and what age students you serve.** We've got to change the mindset and change the neighborhood. I think where it all got started was when we won a literacy grant, a smaller one for about $21,000. The people got all excited when we opened our library and classes. People were excited about coming. Communities like this are willing, but you almost have to serve it to them on a plate. Later, we started a new focus where we brought families in by grade levels to spend a half day with their child and they went together to planned literacy-related events. We did that for the last six years.

3. **What results have you seen at your school that you attribute to hosting family literacy events?** We have been an exemplary campus (state rating on standardized assessment) the last two years. We were so close the last five or six years, missing by a point each time. No doubt in my mind that because of our focus on family literacy, we became an exemplary campus. Our kids have become a little cocky; a nice way to say it is self-esteem. Their self-esteem has risen. They know they are good. Why? Because their parents are involved. They took a chance. They came to school. We made it attractive. We gave them pizza, raffles, and we made it easy for them to come to school. They enjoyed it. We made them feel welcome here. What really happened is what our superintendent, Dr. Steve Flores, calls the "tripod effect." We had the students and the teachers, but what were missing was the parents. The only time the parents would come to school was for PTA (Parent Teacher Association), but that wasn't very successful. We usually had more teachers than

parents at the meetings. This thing was so well planned; it was comfortable and not threatening. It was during the day when our parents could come. I think it was a spark that got family literacy going at our school. Now parents are coming to school more and are actually asking for more.

4. **Were there any surprising results, positive or negative, that you did not expect?** The surprise was how eager they were to come. They've asked for one a week, but we just can't do that. Hopefully, one day we'll get funding to stay open after school and serve the families more. Parent support increased, and they started asking the right questions at parent conferences. In the Hispanic culture and in neighborhoods like this, parents only know one question. "Is my child behaving well?" As soon as the teacher said yes, that was the end of the conference as far as the parent was concerned. Academics were tuned out. Now because we've educated our parents about state assessments, they are beginning to ask about academic things.

5. **Were there any difficulties related to these events that you had to work around?** There were some who only came for the food and would bring guests in time to eat. We worked around that by offering tickets when they signed in at the morning orientation. Those tickets were traded for food at the end.

6. **What kind of parent feedback have you had?** They want more and more. They want the events offered more often, and they want more variety in topics. They are very appreciative of what we are offering them. They'll jokingly say they want a traditional food like *menudo*, a traditional Mexican soup, instead of pizza. Some parents have asked for longer sessions. But, since we include the children, we have to keep their attention spans in mind. We are also using half of the school day for these events, and that's a good amount of time.

7. **What is the basic format of your events?** This year we are going to try something new. Since we did the other format focused on grade levels for six years, this time we are going to offer a list of parent events and topics at the beginning of the school year. Parents will be able to pick and choose the topics they are interested in. For example, we'll do a topic called early reading, which some will like, and other topics will be seasonal. Like during tax season, we'll bring some tax experts in to help the community work on their taxes. During national health awareness times, we'll bring over people to share with our parents. For example, we'll sponsor events during the American Diabetes Month and National Breast Cancer Awareness month. We try to cover social issues as well. We want to keep the focus on instruction, but we're expanding a little by doing this.

8. **Who are the key players in your events? Please include the title of their regular position and the role they play in the events.** Our planning team consists of the librarian, gifted and talented teacher, counselor, reading specialist, and me. We develop a calendar of events for the year and follow a planning sheet that we use for each grade level's event. What the grade level chooses to focus on for their parents is decided by the grade level team with my approval. We run three sessions per event that parents rotate through. There is always a counselor/

nurse session, a reading session, and a grade level session. The librarian and the gifted and talented teacher oversee the events schedule. They announce times for rotation to next groups, oversee sign-ins and raffles, and are the runner to check on each group to see if there are any needs that come up. We also use our parent liaison to provide child care. She finds her own volunteers to help in this area. We are going to experiment next with non–grade level events. We want to provide parents a list of workshops for the year that they can pick and choose from as the year progresses.

9. **How do you pay for these events?** We use some of our budget monies that include areas for parental involvement.

10. **If you were able to speak to other principals who are considering beginning their own family literacy events, what words of advice would you have for them?** These kinds of events are worth the effort. It took some time to get a good schedule worked out, but now it runs smoothly. We saw immediate positive responses from the families. Now, six years later, we are starting to see a better product of student enter our school in kindergarten. Don't forget to provide parent workshops for parents of future students. Teach the parents how to work with their toddlers and preschoolers now. It'll pay off for you. Our parents are a lot more involved now than they have ever been before. They are more comfortable coming to us for help because we have consistently reached out to them in other areas.

FAMILY LITERACY SCHOOL LIBRARIAN INTERVIEW

Name: Nancy (a retired librarian)

1. **How do you define Family Literacy?** Family Literacy is the cooperative efforts of school personnel, parents, and their community to promote and increase academic, social, and economic success (graduation+) for students and their families.

2. **What caused you to pursue family literacy events for your school? Please include how long you have participated in providing these events and what age students you serve.** My campus had glaring needs; 96% of the students were economically disadvantaged and many of their parents had never graduated from high school. Our entry level reading test scores were very low, and it was a struggle to raise our students to passing level on our high stakes state assessments.

    Our campus began a partnership with KMBH Public TV station and their Ready to Learn Coordinator who with me, the librarian, began parent-focused sessions once a month, targeting our pre-K thru second-grade parents. Later we expanded with the Improving Literacy through School Libraries Grant, adding afterschool activities for the students and once a month Saturday family (students and their parents) literacy activities.

3. **What results have you seen at your school that you attribute to hosting family literacy events?** Increased parental involvement in school activities, increased parent use of our library materials/services, increased student circulation of materials in the library, increased number of "words read" by our student body. As well, our reading and writing scores on the state assessments for grades 3–5 improved.

4. **Were there any surprising results, positive or negative, that you did not expect?** There was an overwhelming response of students who wanted to participate in afterschool activities.

   Shy, reluctant parents showed an increase in confidence; several parents sought jobs and were hired at local businesses enabling students to see their parents in this new working role. Some parents became weekly volunteers at our campus, boosting the confidence of their students.

   Most surprising was the beginning of a campus Chess Team five years ago. For the last three years, this chess team has earned the honor of competing not only at the state level but the national level. Of course this has boosted school spirit, but more importantly it has worked wonders for some individual chess players and their families. Some had previously been troubled, under-achieving students, and they became highly respected for their chess skills, improved behavior, and academic success.

5. **Were there any difficulties related to these events that you had to work around?** Our target group of parents was initially reluctant to participate. We kept inviting, inviting, and inviting them to events. We found coupons for free books and used door prizes (donated by staff) to help bring the parents to school. Once a few came, word of mouth about their positive experiences helped bring in more parents.

6. **What kind of parent feedback have you had?** Because our campus is several miles from the public library, many parents are regular patrons of my library, coming to check out books and media before and after school for their younger, preschool children. To me, that is the highest level of success for Family Literacy.

7. **What is the basic format of your events?** Our campus started with three basic literacy formats. One was for parents only, giving monthly sessions highlighting tips for student academic success. A second format was for students only; afterschool literacy activities in the library and campus computer labs. A third format was monthly family events where students and their parents could explore activities in a certain subject area. We hosted math, science, literature, as well as "Build a Book" events.

   Our campus has recently added a fourth literacy format; career awareness for our third through fifth grade students. We have invited guest speakers to share information about their professions with our girls during the "Women in Heels" program and with our boys during the "Men in Black" program. We also arrange a field trip to an area college/university for our fifth graders.

8. **Who are the key players in your events? Please include the title of their regular position and the role they play in the events.**
Campus Coordinator of all Literacy Events: Campus Librarian
Parent Trainers:

> Ready to Learn Coordinator from local public television station
> Campus Librarian, myself
> Pre-Kindergarten Teacher

Supervisors/Facilitators for Student Literacy Activities:

> Campus Librarian
> Teachers from Pre-K thru Third Grade
> Computer Lab Paraprofessional

Family Day Facilitators: Volunteer teachers from our campus, all grade levels
Coordinator /Speakers/ Hosts for Career Days: Principal

> Counselor
> Community Leaders and Businessmen/women
> Campus Librarian
> Local College Professors

9. **How do you pay for these events?** We began with grants; Ready to Learn and then the biggest grant, Improving Literacy through School Libraries. Once my principal realized the success of our programs, she began finding monies to help fund literacy activities on campus.

10. **If you were able to speak to other school librarians who are considering beginning their own family literacy events, what words of advice would you have for them?** Seek the support of your campus administrators, counselors, and teachers. For a campus to have a successful family literacy program everyone on the campus needs to buy into the concept and be willing to help.
Apply for grants, contact local community leaders and businessmen for financial support or volunteer services or goods.

   If funding looks bleak, you may try to work with existing programs (PTA, afterschool programs, district or campus parental involvement programs, public libraries) and help them enlarge their literacy vision and at the same time promote your library.

11. **Additional comments:** Yes, it takes extra time and effort to coordinate literacy activities, but it is so rewarding when you see individual students and individual families refocus on academic success! It is also gratifying to know your principal sees and understands what you, the librarian, have contributed to the high stakes test scores! It could also mean job security at a time when education budgets are being cut nationwide.

FAMILY LITERACY READING SPECIALIST INTERVIEW

Name: Diana Morales

My objective was to offer parents ideas as to how they could help their children at home in the area of reading. Some of my colleagues would present other topics. Many parents wanted to help, but they didn't know specifically how to begin, or they were unaware that they had much to offer in their child's education. Many parents felt that because they came from Mexico and couldn't speak English, they would not be able to help. One of our main goals was to reassure parents that the school belonged to them and that they were an important part of our school. I began my presentation by introducing myself, letting them know how long I'd been teaching as well as giving them my educational background and telling them about how the children were selected for my critical skills classes as a classroom support teacher where my classes helped children to catch up with the other students.

First, I had to plan how I could effectively help parents as I gathered information for my PowerPoint. Next, I prepared a PowerPoint presentation about what I felt every parent needed to know. I added animated clip art with animation and sound effects to keep the children's attention. I decided the parent and child should have some interactive activity to work on together. This part has changed throughout the many years I have presented. Initially, I used to have learning games that they could work on together. Later, our school hired a new certified librarian, purchased more library computers, and updated our books through a grant we had split between three schools. I wanted to feature our student's independence in reading and show off their ability by taking AR tests on their own. After my PowerPoint presentation, the parents would listen to their child read AR books. Parents could try out the different levels of questions I had talked about prior to this.

Afterwards the child would proceed to the computer and take a test as the parents would watch. Perhaps that isn't a big deal at your school, but for us it is. Very few students had computers at that time. The majority of families still don't have them. Some of the families that do have computers had participated in a drawing where our fifth graders had won old computers that we were replacing or had been donated by a long-time HOSTS (Helping One Student To Succeed) mentor. It just so happened that one of our mentors had relatives that had owned a private school up north. This couple decided to close their private school, and our students were the fortunate recipients of a raffle for their leftover computers. All of these raffles had to be approved by our superintendent.

I have done presentations for each grade level in the primary grades. For kindergarten you may want to include concepts about print and other skills that students need such as making sound boxes, clapping syllables, developing oral language through nursery rhymes, chants, finger plays, etc. Encourage parents to hold their children in their lap or read to them before going to sleep. Some ideas you may want to encourage are:

1. Label child's name on bedroom door as well as toys and belongings for name recognition.
2. Sing alphabet song and have child point to the letters.
3. Purchase alphabet books to expand vocabulary.
4. Use magnetic letters on refrigerator door.
5. Make alphabet book by folding sheets of paper and label each page with alphabet then periodically cut pictures from magazines and newspapers. Try to coordinate with the sound for the week that is being introduced at school.
6. Choose books with pattern or repetitive text.
7. Have student name parts of the book and words such as title, author, and illustrator, and ask child what jobs the author and illustrator do.
8. Point to words as you read to encourage one-to-one matching of spoken words to print.
9. Ask basic questions after reading to determine how much the child really comprehended. Ask questions such as: Who are the main characters? What was the problem? What was the solution? Retell the story: What happened at the beginning? The middle? The end? Encourage oral language development by expecting children to respond in complete sentences.
10. Obtain public library cards and encourage weekly visits as well as showing respect and handling of books by turning pages correctly.
11. To make a book fun and memorable, make products using household objects. Example: marshmallow snowman; paper bag puppet to retell story to encourage sequencing; glue beans, macaroni, or rice to make the shape of a character, etc.

Since we began, each grade levels had a theme. My PowerPoint pictures reflected that theme. For example, first grade themes have been Camp Read A Lot (I used camping pictures in my PowerPoint); then it became First Grade Is Reaching for the Stars (I used pictures about space). When we reached exemplary status, it became Engage, Explore, and Exemplary, which was a district motto; and later Camp Ready to Read (I used navigation as a theme). I think you get the idea. The information for that grade was basically the same, but the pictures and sounds went with the theme. Second grade usually had their parent meetings during the fall season. One theme became Harvest a Future for Your Children. Another was Fall into Learning with appropriate pictures and sounds. These are just a few examples.

Debriefing as a team: After one of these events, the entire team would meet for lunch in the conference room and discuss what had transpired throughout the sessions. We would also read the evaluations in English and Spanish. Mostly they were very complimentary and some had very good suggestions as to what else they would like to see in future presentations. Some of our parents spoke only Spanish and a few were illiterate. Some parents had short attentions spans and were really there for the pizza or because their child expected them to go. Others would not shut off their cell phones, and still others refused to take their toddlers to the child care room when they started to cry. These were some of the problems we had not anticipated. We made adjustments along the way and learned more each time as to how it would run more efficiently. Through persistence and careful planning, our sessions became better each time.

Some of the resources I used were *Beginning Reading Instruction: Practical Ideas for Parents* from the Texas Education Agency. Another was *Estrategias y actividades para acelerar la lectura de estudiantes que no leen al nivel apropriado* from Region IV in cooperation with the Texas Education Agency. Manuals from the *Texas Teacher's Reading Academy I and II* were another valuable resource. I also used Reading Recovery strategies. Teachers can go through these ideas and be selective about activities that parents can do at home or the types of comprehension questions they can ask. I also translated all PowerPoints and handouts for our Spanish-speaking parents as needed.

FAMILY LITERACY CHILDREN'S BOOK STORE OWNER INTERVIEW

Name: Sarah A. Cuadra (owner of Storybook Garden)

1. **How do you define Family Literacy?** Books in the home; parent(s) that read and demonstrate love of reading/books/learning; bedtime stories; trips to a bookstore/library; participation in community literary/arts events.

2. **What caused you to get involved in family literacy? Please include how long you have participated in providing these events and what age students you serve.** I've always had a love for learning, reading, and books; my mother taught me that a book can take you to many places, and if you can read, you can do anything. I opened an indie children's bookshop nearly 10 years ago. I have also been the dyslexia specialist for the last six years at the school where I teach.

3. **What results have you seen that you attribute to hosting family literacy events?** Happy children and happy parents! They want to come back and participate again. They say things like, "That was great. Let's do that again."

4. **Were there any surprising results, positive or negative, that you did not expect?** The turnout varies depending on the event. Sometimes we may have more people turnout for a costume character instead of attending an author event.

5. **Were there any difficulties related to these events that you had to work around?** Not really. Perhaps running out of books could be viewed as a problem, but it is really a good thing.

6. **What kind of feedback have you had?** Positive and encouraging.

7. **What is the basic format of your events?** If it's a book signing: Welcome, Introduction, Feature, Questions & Answers, Book Signing, and Photo Opportunities.

8. **Who are the key players in your events? Please include the title of their regular position and the role they play in the events.** Sarah & Juan—Owners; my mother and sisters if needed for additional support (crowd control, cash register help); our

10-year-old daughter—she's the photographer for events. These are family-run events.

9. **How are the events paid for?** We really don't have any expenses, but when we do, the money comes from event/supply budget.

10. **If you were able to speak to other book store owners who are considering beginning their own family literacy events, what words of advice would you have for them?** Be creative and keep your costs to little or nothing so you can stay in business and have many more future events.

INDEX

ABOUT THE AUTHORS

Dr. ROSEMARY CHANCE is an assistant professor in the department of library science at Sam Houston State University. Before teaching at the university level, she worked as a school librarian for 14 years. She earned a PhD in library science from Texas Woman's University in Denton, Texas. Her most recent publication is *Young Adult Literature in Action: A Librarian's Guide* (2008), part of the Library and Information Science Text Series published by Libraries Unlimited.

Dr. LAURA SHENEMAN is the coordinator of library services for Harlingen CISD, in Harlingen, Texas. Prior to this she taught in the library science department of Sam Houston State University. Her 20 years in education also include serving as an elementary school librarian and classroom teacher. She earned her EdD in curriculum and instruction from the University of Houston with a dual emphasis in teacher preparation and instructional technology.